WHAT PEOPLE ARE SAYING ABOUT "DISCOVERING THE FATHER'S HEART"

"In Discovering His Heart, Timothy Saipramuk has woven the tapestry of his journey to healing which started with a desire to quench unanswered questions, leading to a revelation which eludes many people, that being Jesus' place in our lives. In his poetic style of writing, he was able to show the reader how he turned reflection into meaning. He shows how surrendering enabled him to "encounter the deep truth that Jesus is the way-the path to self-discovery, redemption, and transformative growth". Timothy created for himself a textbook example of what it looks like to go from trauma to healing, from family to divorce, to homelessness, to depression, and finally to redemption and healing. If you find yourself in these pages, don't stop reading. There is hope. "

– BILL YAICH

"In Tim's 1st book, he bravely shares his inspiring story of moving through his personal tragedy & showing how the unexpected events in our lives can be paths to spiritual health, healing & joy!"

– BARBARA BURICA

"Reading like a well-worded novel, the journey of a man's loss, from divorce to near suicide, reveals that redemption and restoration is the divine plan. Well, lined with scriptures, God's words supported the steps and uplifted this man from the depths. This book is an excellent companion for the one in the midst of a devasting divorce or searching for solid ground, the

rock on which to stand when everything around in life seems to be crumbling."

– LARISA PALAZZOLO

"After immersing myself in the pages of this book, my emotions were stirred in ways I never expected. Each sentence resonated with me, echoing thoughts and feelings I've experienced myself. The journey from darkness to light, guided by faith and divine intervention, mirrored my own struggles and triumphs. This book has reignited my passion for spirituality, reminding me of the constant presence of God in our lives. It inspired me to embrace courage and seek help when needed, bringing me enormous joy and peace. The author's words have become a daily mantra, guiding me to surrender control and find comfort in God's embrace. I am grateful to have encountered such a sincere work and eagerly anticipate the continued journey it has ignited within me. You are truly amazing, and I am so blessed to call you, my friend."

– JOJO REED

"I love your book! So many insights into the weave and weft of such a personal journey. Perfect for anyone whose faith is being tried by circumstances and is tired of hearing all those well-meaning quotes that seem to gloss over the pain. Having also gone through divorce, but as the initiator, it was beautiful to read your experience and still painful. The understanding of how God works things for our good, using the pain to find and fill the cracks as we allow Him to refine us is not meant to make everything "peachy". It's meant to create beauty *without* glossing over the brokenness. The shards are still there, and there can still be aches - allowing Him to re-work us into a piece of art out of those pieces, like stained glass, displays the brokenness and the beauty. His heart is for our good, our healing, and for the greater good and healing."

– BELEN HARRIS

"Timothy Saipramuk, with a very unique, metaphorical writing style, takes us on a journey to the depths of his soul's despair to surrender to His heavenly Father. He found that no matter how far he had strayed, the Father's heart awaited his return. This prodigal returned home, discovering His Father's Heart and the true purpose of his life. Anyone reading this book will find reflection of areas in his or her own heart, as well. May God use this written work to reach many tired "souls" with encouragement and hope."

– LINDA GROSS

"Wow, what an amazing read! You actually feel as if you are living Timothy's experience as you unfold the pages of text. His raw, honest, and authentic style of writing really evokes an emotional response to the story. Such pain, such suffering, what a testimony of love, mercy and grace from our Father, His Heart is so big! He loves us so much! This is a must read! It is chock full of scripture & details - a true story of redemption & faith! It is inspiring & will have you anticipating the next chapter as you walk in Timothy's shoes while he is Discovering His Heart! glory to God in the Highest! Thank you for sharing, Timothy. I know God is leading you in your journey, and His Holy Spirit is over you & your beautiful children. God bless you friend."

– JEN BRYAN

"Reading Discovering the Father's Heart is like being transported straight into the scenes Tim describes. He has such *a rare gift for creative writing—his words don't just tell you something, they take you there. The detail is so vivid you feel the weight of every moment, the tension of every trial, and the beauty of every breakthrough. It's as if he's a film director, not only writing the script but also capturing the soundtrack underneath it all, so you feel exactly what the story is meant to stir in you. Watching his journey as he's written this book has been nothing short of epic. We all have a story, but what sets Tim's apart isn't just the hardship he's walked through—it's the choices he's made along the way. Choices to humble himself, to seek the Creator, and to exchange pain for presence. And you can see it in every chapter: he has truly found the heart of the Father, and now his own heart beats for nothing more. That's what makes this book powerful. It's not just words—it's a life surrendered. And that surrender has shaped him into the man and father he is today. Not perfect, but yielded. Not flawless, but faithful. And it shows in how he loves his children, how he serves, and how he tells this story. The timing of the book's completion couldn't have been more prophetic. After writing the manuscript in just four months, it took nearly a year to finalize. The original cover showed a caterpillar, with the subtitle "A War Within a Father's Heart." But on September 4, 2025—while making the final edits—something shifted. The caterpillar disappeared, and what replaced it was a tangerine tree. The subtitle became: From Wilderness Wandering to Orchard Rebirth. That day, Tim also experienced a deeply healing moment, finally giving voice to the pain of his childhood—where culture had silenced his feelings. I watched the Creator Himself uproot that old lie, and in its place came FREEDOM. A wall came down. Roots were removed. And just like the new cover design, his own life was testifying to what this book declares: when roots are healed, fruit begins to grow.*

The fact that the symbol of a tangerine tree surfaced on the very day he finalized the book is no accident. It ties back to a sacred memory with his father under a clementine tree before he passed in Thailand. And it ties forward to the fruitfulness Yahweh is now birthing out of Tim's life. This is not just a book—it's a living testimony. I couldn't be prouder of him. For his courage to write. For his obedience to share. For his humility to keep choosing the Father's heart above all else. And for the way his story now becomes a mirror for others who are longing to discover the same freedom. If you've ever wrestled with identity, fatherhood, loss, or the wilderness seasons of life—this book will meet you there. And it won't leave you there. This isn't just a story. It's a rebirth."

– JEN HORLING

DISCOVERING THE FATHER'S HEART

FROM WILDERNESS WANDERING TO ORCHARD REBIRTH

TIMOTHY SAIPRAMUK

Copyright © 2025 Timothy Saipramuk
All Rights Reserved. No part of this book may be reproduced in any form or by any electronic or mechanical means, including information storage and retrieval systems, without permission in writing from the publisher, except by reviewers, who may quote brief passages in a review.

Thank you for your honor in helping protect author's rights.

Discovering The Father's Heart
From Wilderness Wandering To Orchard Rebirth

ISBN: 978-1-7349204-2-0
Printed in the United States of America

Cover Design by: Sponge Designs, Inc

www.theovercomersmovement.com

DEDICATION

Praise to Yahweh for the gift in *Discovering the Father's Heart*

For four years, I walked through the wilderness of confusion, wrestling with failure, regret, and the weight of my past. I left behind my two children, Ethan and Charlotte, in the aftermath of divorce, and I struggled to piece my life back together. I fell—again and again. But through it all, You never left me. When I was lost, You guided me. When I was broken, You held me. When I questioned my worth, You reminded me that I was Yours.

It was in the fire that You refined me. In my darkest moments, You brought clarity. In my weakness, You proved Yourself strong. I now stand not because of my own strength, but because of Your grace. My failures did not define me—You did. My past did not disqualify me—You restored me.

This book is my offering of gratitude, a declaration that You alone are worthy. May every word written here reflect Your goodness, Your faithfulness, and Your power to redeem. Let my story serve as a witness to those who feel lost, broken, or unworthy—that You are the Creator who restores, who calls, and who never forsakes His children. To You, Yahweh, be all the glory. Forever and always.

Discovering His Heart

TABLE OF CONTENTS

Introduction — 19
Unanswered Questions and Unspoken Goodbyes

Chapter 1 — 35
I Will Never Say Goodbye

Chapter 2 — 47
The Threshold of the Unknown

Chapter 3 — 59
The Detour into Darkness

Chapter 4 — 69
The Weight of Return

Chapter 5 — 77
The Road That Carried My Sorrow

Chapter 6 — 87
The Road Remembers

Chapter 7 — 97
Laughter, Love, and Silent Goodbyes

Chapter 8 — 105
The Promise That Never Breaks

Chapter 9 — 115
Monuments of What Once Was

Chapter 10 — 123
A Love That Had Been Waiting

Chapter 11 — 133
The Question That Could Have Saved Me

Chapter 12 — 143
Unraveling the Storm Within

Chapter 13   153
Forged in Fire: Turning Pain into Power

Chapter 14   165
A Life in Motion, A Soul at Rest

Chapter 15   173
Borrowed Time, Borrowed Spaces

Chapter 16   181
Battles Fought in the Dark

Chapter 17   189
Not Answers, but Understanding

Chapter 18   199
The Tunnel of Endless Night

Chapter 19   209
Brotherhood in the Mountains

Chapter 20   217
The Currency of Compassion.

Chapter 21   229
Lessons from the Tangerine Tree (RIP – September 10, 1995)

Chapter 22   237
The Dismantling of a Kingdom

Chapter 23   253
The Sacred Surrender

Bio   273

Discovering His Heart

Discovering His Heart

INTRODUCTION
UNANSWERED QUESTIONS AND UNSPOKEN GOODBYES

The sun blazed overhead as I navigated the winding roads from Southern California to Covelo, my mind preoccupied with the miles ahead. My phone buzzed, and Christina's name flashed across the screen. Assuming it was a family matter—an emergency demanding my immediate attention—I answered without hesitation.

Little did I know that this drive home would be marked by a revelation that would alter the course of my life.

Christina's text urged me to make a detour to an office in Santa Rosa for paperwork. Expecting some urgent family issue, I complied, my thoughts racing with concern. But when I arrived, the truth blindsided me. The paperwork in question was not about our children, a shared responsibility, or even a logistical issue, it was my own divorce papers.

The weight of the revelation pressed down on me as a receptionist led me into a muted conference room. The air was thick with unspoken emotions, the silence stretching between the walls like an invisible force. The atmosphere buzzed with tension as I took my seat across from Christina's lawyer—a woman who, until this moment, had been nothing more than a distant name.

Her demeanor was measured, professional, yet the faint trace of a knowing smile betrayed the gravity of the moment. This was not just a conversation. It was the moment my marriage officially ended, the threshold between what was and what would never be again.

As she methodically sorted through the paperwork, the

rhythmic rustling of pages played like the soundtrack to a life unraveling. Each sheet carried the weight of finality, its crisp edges marking the slow but steady march toward dissolution. The ink, bold and unwavering, held the power to redefine everything I once knew—my role as a husband, the structure of my family, the foundation of the life we had built together.

Her smile, though formal, carried an unspoken understanding—a quiet acknowledgment of the gravity of this moment. It was not just a transaction; it was an emotional reckoning, the closing of a door that had once led to shared dreams and promises. There was something unsettling in that smile, a recognition that within these sterile legal formalities lay the raw, unfiltered weight of human relationships breaking apart.

As I stared at the paperwork before me, I realized it was more than just legal documents. It was a tangible manifestation of the intangible—the end of a chapter I had never anticipated closing. A story that had once felt certain was now veering into uncharted, unexpected territory, leaving me to navigate the next steps alone.

As I mechanically signed my portion, the pen moved with a weight that went beyond ink and paper. Each stroke carried the finality of a life once intertwined, marking not just the completion of a legal process but the emotional punctuation of a shared journey.

The pen's path across the page mirrored the path I had walked in this relationship—one that I had once believed would stretch into forever. Yet, with each signature, the illusion of continuity faded, replaced by the stark reality of an ending. The ink traced the lines of finality, closing a chapter that had once been filled with dreams, whispered vows, and a future envisioned together.

It was the last note of a symphony that had once played in harmony, now fading into silence.

After leaving the lawyer's office, I found comfort in my pickup truck. The door's creak shut behind me, sealing off the echoes of legal discussions and the weight of an irreversible decision. Inside the cabin, reality settled in with an undeniable force. I took a deep breath, allowing the moment to sink in.

The divorce papers, now tucked away, were more than just documents—they were the final punctuation on a chapter that had endured both storms and celebrations. The gravity of it all pressed against me, and in that small space, the truck became more than just a vehicle; it became a cocoon of reflection.

The hum of the engine filled the silence, a steady backdrop to the turbulence within. The soft glow of the dashboard lights illuminated the truth I could no longer escape—this truck, once a vessel of shared road trips, laughter, and everyday life, now carried only one soul, navigating a future that felt uncertain and uncharted.

In that moment of silence, I instinctively reached for my phone, searching for something—someone—to steady me in the sea of uncertainty. The familiar name of my sister, Pon, illuminated the screen, a small but powerful reminder that I was not entirely alone.

As soon as I heard her voice, a soothing balm to my troubled thoughts, the weight pressing against my chest eased, if only slightly. She became my anchor, grounding me when everything else felt like it was slipping away. The call, though just words carried through a signal, felt like a lifeline—tethering me to a world that, in that moment, seemed to be fading into the distance.

Pon, wise and empathetic, listened patiently as I poured out the tangled emotions and complexities of the situation. Her voice, steady and sure, cut through my confusion with the clarity of experience. She urged me to seek answers—not just vague reassurances, but direct, pointed questions that would serve as a crucible test for the fate of my marriage. Her words did not offer comfort in the traditional sense, but they gave me something more valuable in that moment—a sense of purpose amid the chaos.

With renewed focus, I turned the key in the ignition, and the engine roared to life, breaking the heavy silence that had settled around me. As I pulled away from the lawyer's office, the road ahead stretched into uncertainty, its distant horizon holding answers I was not sure I was ready to face. The headlights of my pickup truck pierced the darkness, illuminating a path that was both daunting and unexplored.

As I gripped the steering wheel, I felt the weight of both the literal and metaphorical journey ahead. With every mile back to Covelo, I was not just returning home—I was stepping into the storm of emotions and revelations that lay ahead, determined to navigate them with whatever strength I had left.

The wheels of my pickup truck hummed in steady rhythm as I embarked on the hour-and-thirty-minute drive back to Covelo. Inside the cabin, a reflective silence filled the space, stretching endlessly before me like the road itself. The asphalt unraveled beneath me, winding through familiar landscapes that blurred into the background as my mind wrestled with the weight of this new reality.

Emotions surged like a relentless storm, thoughts circling in an endless loop, searching for the reasons behind the collapse of my marriage. Each curve in the road seemed to mirror the highs and lows of our unraveling, the twists and turns echoing the chaos of love lost.

Glancing in the rearview mirror, I caught sight of a face lined with reflection—eyes staring into the distance, searching for answers that refused to surface. The silence within the truck was deafening, a quiet reflection of the storm inside me. Questions loomed large, and answers remained just out of reach, dancing in the periphery like shadows cast by the headlights. The hurricane of emotions—confusion, sorrow, regret—raged within, mirroring the uncertainty of the road stretching ahead.

Discovering His Heart

The landscape of Covelo unfolded before me like the pages of a bittersweet novel, each tree and familiar landmark carrying the weight of shared memories.

As I approached, Christina stood on the lots, a solitary silhouette engraved against the canvas of our shared history. The air, thick with unspoken emotions, seemed to hum with the echoes of conversations, laughter, and moments that now belonged to the past.

After parking, I took a moment to gather my thoughts before stepping into the emotional terrain that lay ahead. The soft crunch of gravel beneath my shoes seemed to echo in the stillness of the surroundings, intensifying the gravity of the awaiting conversation. The landscape, once a backdrop to moments of joy and togetherness, now stood witness to a turning point that would redefine the course of our relationship.

As I approached Christina, her silhouette held a certain expression against the fading light of the day. The driveway, once a symbol of shared dreams and a future seen together, now stood as a silent witness to the complexities that had shattered our connection. The air between us felt charged with emotion, each step towards her a response to the storm waiting to be navigated. Christina's words, spoken with gravity that echoed in the quiet of the afternoon, hung in the air like a conclusive verdict.

"It's already done."

The weight of those words settled on my shoulders, signaling that the course of our journey had permanently shifted. The landscape, once a haven, now marked an emotional crossroads. The fading light painted an image of emotions—the shadows cast by the trees mirrored the complexities of our shared history. The driveway, once a place of unity, now seemed to stretch endlessly, underscoring the emotional distance that had grown between us. The moment hung suspended in time, a pause before the inevitable, as we stood on the threshold of a conversation that would reshape the landscape of our relationship.

The door to the house swung open, and the moment I stepped inside, a tidal wave of energy crashed into me. My children, the purest reflections of innocence and joy, charged forward with uncontainable excitement. Their little feet pounded against the floor, their laughter ringing through the hallway as they threw their arms around me, wrapping me in the warmth of their embrace.

For a brief, fleeting moment, the storm of emotions that had followed me home was silenced. In their hugs, I found a temporary refuge—a sanctuary untouched by the weight of legal documents, unanswered questions, and an uncertain future. Here, in their boundless love, I felt something I had not in a long time—home.

Later that evening, with the children tucked into beds, the house settled into a hush, the air still carrying the echoes of bedtime stories and lullabies. The gentle grow of nightlights softened the room, concealing the unspoken tension that lingered. I approached Christina, suggesting we step out onto the front lawn for a conversation filled with unspoken truths.

As we sat beneath the canvas of the night sky, two chairs, positioned with a physical distance that mirrored the emotional gap between us silently reflecting the unspoken words between us. Though physically separated, the emotional mess remained; the space between us was but an illusion. The front lawn, beneath the watchful gaze of stars, once a symbol of intimacy, now served as the backdrop for the redefinition of our relationship—a conversation marked by the echoes of shared memories and the unspoken acceptance that the path ahead would be walked separately.

In the stillness of the night, as shadows danced across the front lawn, I struggled to voice my thoughts, the words faltered under the weight of conflicting emotions. Christina, a silent witness to my internal battle, met my gaze with a depth that spoke of the weight of our shared history. Her eyes, windows to a journey we had traveled together, held a vulnerability just beneath the surface. It was as if the unspoken nuances of our connection were etched in the lines and creases of her expression.

Breaking the silence, Christina's voice, cut through the stillness of the night.

"Two people don't have to be married to still love each other."

The words hung in the air like a fragile thread, weaving a narrative that challenged the traditional boundaries of marriage. Confusion flickered across my face, mirroring the complexity of redefining our relationship. Seeking clarity, I leaned in, trying to grasp her perspective. The stillness of the night only amplified the weight of the unspoken question between us.

"Do you believe people grow apart as they get older?" she asked.

For me, the idea that people could grow apart felt unimaginable, a notion that clashed with the foundation of our connection. As I tried to articulate our unique journey, the words carried the weight of conviction in a shared story that spanned the full spectrum of life's highs and lows.

"Maybe for others, but not for us," I responded. "We were together since I had nothing, and now we have everything,"

The silence that followed spoke volumes, heavy with unspoken truths. It was a moment of quiet reflection, an unspoken recognition that words alone could not bridge the gaps that had formed between us. Christina's gaze, layered with emotion, revealed her own thoughts, leaving an unanswered question hanging in the night air.

In a desperate attempt to make sense of our unraveling, I pleaded with Christina for clarity.

"Can you tell me what I've done wrong in our marriage, as

a man, as a husband, and as a father, so I can be better for the future?"

The question asked with raw sincerity, sought more than just an explanation—it searched for a path to growth and redemption. Its weight settled between us, a shared burden demanding honesty and vulnerability. Christina's response, spoken with quiet finality, cut through the night air, leaving an undeniable truth hanging between us.

"It's not my job to tell you; it's your job to find out for yourself," she declared, her words cutting through the quiet like a chilling wind.

It was a cold truth, a revelation that added yet another layer of complexity to the already intricate tapestry of our conversation. The silence that followed became an abyss— an unbridgeable chasm stretching between us, heavy with unspoken words. In its depths, the weight of unanswered questions lingered, casting an uneasy stillness over the night. What was once a canvas for shared dreams and whispered confidence now bore witness to the fraying threads of a connection strained by unspoken truths.

As we retreated into the house, the door closed behind us with a finality that echoed the unanswered questions still hanging in the air. The space between us seemed to stretch wider, each step burdened by the weight of a conversation left incomplete. The walls, once witnesses to the symphony of our shared life, now stood as silent sentinels to the growing distance between us.

Inside, the silence persisted, thick and suffocating, wrapping around us like a heavy cloak. The unanswered questions became ghosts, haunting the corners of our home, lingering in every unspoken moment. Christina and I, disconnected by the weight of words left unsaid, moved through the rooms like strangers, uncertain and adrift. The weight of the night settled on our shoulders, leaving us to navigate its consequences in the quiet that draped the house like a shroud.

As the night deepened, I sought refuge in our children's room, their peaceful sleep a bittersweet comfort before me. The soft glow of nightlights bathed the space in warmth, a serene sanctuary untouched by the turmoil weighing on my heart. Once a place of bedtime stories and whispered lullabies, the room now bore silent witness to the quiet unraveling of our family.

Watching them sleep, their innocence reflected in their dream faces, my heart ached with guilt. The reality settled in—soon, they would no longer feel the steady presence of my warmth before bedtime or wake to the familiar comfort of my figure in the morning. The cherished rituals of bedtime hugs and whispered goodnights, once a source of joy, now felt like poignant reminders of a bond slipping through my fingers.

This nightly journey of love and regret became a ritual—an emotional passage through the maze of my own heart. The room, adorned with remnants of their laughter and the echoes of shared stories, offered a fragile refuge from the storm outside. Yet, each night, as I stood on the precipice of separation, the weight in my chest grew heavier.

Guilt, ever-present, lingered in the corners of my mind as I watched their steady breaths in the stillness. The looming absence hovered silently over their sleeping forms, an unspoken presence in the dim glow of the night. Their innocence, untouched by the turmoil within me, stood in stark contrast to the storm I carried, creating a poignant tapestry of love, sorrow, and longing.

This nightly ritual—a delicate dance between love and regret—played out in the quiet shadows of their room. What was once a sanctuary of warmth and connection had become a bittersweet reminder of the void creeping into our lives, soon to echo through the bedtime routine that once bound us together.

And then came the final night—a night burdened with the weight of the last goodbyes. As I stood in the doorway, the room seemed to hold its breath, as if it, too, understood the significance of this moment. This was the last time I would stand here, watching my children sleep in peaceful innocence.

The dim glow of the nightlights cast long shadows, stretching into an unknown future where our bedtime rituals would exist only in memory. In that heartbreaking silence, surrounded by the rhythmic breaths of my sleeping children, I carried the weight of an unspoken farewell.

The room, once alive with laughter, bedtime stories, and whispered "I love you," now stood still—a silent witness to the inevitability of change and the ache of unsaid goodbyes.

The impact of that evening's conversation with Christina rippled through time, marking a turning point I had yet to fully grasp. Her question lingered like an unanswered prayer: "Can you tell me what I've done wrong in our marriage, as a man, as a husband, and as a father, so I can be better for the future?" Her response—a cryptic statement—echoed in my mind like a riddle waiting to be unraveled: "It's not my job to tell you; it's your job to find out for yourself."

In the wake of her words, my days, months, and years became an unrelenting search for answers. I immersed myself in books, sought wisdom from mentors, and sat through counseling sessions, all in pursuit of clarity. I dissected every moment, every decision, every flaw, desperate to uncover the blind spots that had led us here. Yet, despite the guidance, the reflections, and the relentless self-examination, the truth remained just out of reach—slipping through my fingers like grains of sand.

As I navigated the depths of self-analysis, an unshakable void echoed within—an emptiness that no amount of worldly wisdom or conventional advice could fill. Despite my exhaustive search for answers, the subtle nudges of providence began to emerge, gently steering me toward an unexpected truth. Every path I pursued, every piece of well-intentioned counsel I followed, seemed to converge on a single, undeniable realization—Yahweh held the answers to the questions haunting my soul.

What began as a desperate quest for self-improvement—for understanding my role as a man, a husband, and a father—ultimately led me to the only place where true transformation could occur: in cultivating a personal relationship with Him.

But the journey toward spiritual surrender was neither immediate nor simple. It stretched over four years of wrestling with my own shortcomings, battling the weight of my failures, and slowly learning to find refuge in Him. Then, on the sacred evening of August 21, 2023, I reached the pinnacle of my journey of submission. In an act of complete surrender, I bowed at His feet, acknowledging that the answers I had long sought were not found in human understanding but in His infinite grace—the wellspring of all wisdom.

CHAPTER 1
I WILL NEVER SAY GOODBYES

The first light of dawn broke the darkness, streaking the sky with hues of gold—a quiet declaration of a day that felt both peaceful and uncertain. As I stirred awake, the weight of impending change settled over me, shadowing the familiar rhythm of my morning routine. The sun, like a gentle intruder, crept through the curtains, casting a warm glow over the room. Everything felt the same, yet different, charged with an unspoken anticipation, as if even the walls knew this day held the promise of transformation.

As I moved through the motions of my morning, the routine unfolded like an elegant dance, each step familiar, yet laced with deeper meaning. Folding back the covers felt symbolic, as if peeling back the layers of my own life, exposing truths I could no longer ignore. The gentle gurgle of the coffee machine played its usual melody, a steady rhythm in a world shifting beneath my feet.

With each sip, the warmth of the coffee tethered me to the past, offering brief solace in the face of the unknown. The steam rising from the cup carried whispers of resilience, a quiet assurance that even in the midst of change, some things remained constant. The interplay of routine, morning light, and the scent of coffee wove together a delicate tapestry—one that held both the ache of transition and the quiet hope of continuity.

As I moved through the quiet morning, an unexpected encounter with my ex-wife's parents added another weight to the already heavy atmosphere. The air between us felt thick, charged with unspoken words that neither side dared to voice. Once, their gazes had been warm, filled with familiarity and shared history. Now, they carried a passive distance, acknowledging my presence, yet withholding the closeness that had once existed.

As they passed by on their way to work, the silence between us spoke louder than any words could. It was not just a casual exchange; it was a quiet reckoning, a moment filled with the lingering emotions of a relationship that had unraveled. The weight of what had been—and what was now lost—hung in the air like an echo, fading with each step they took away from me.

My ex-wife's mother, once a pillar of kindness, broke the silence with a fleeting smile—a fragile expression, as delicate as a wisp of smoke. It lingered only for a moment, carrying an unspoken wish that I simply cease to exist in their world. Beneath its surface lay a quiet battle, an attempt to balance past affection with present pain, to uphold the appearance of respect while wrestling with the rawness of loss.

In that instant, I felt the weight of history pressing down on us—the struggle to reconcile what had been with what could never be again. The tension settled into the quiet morning, weaving itself into the fabric of the day, setting the stage for a farewell that would fracture the heart one final time.

Each step I took echoed with the remnants of what once was—a family, a lifetime of shared moments, and a connection that had slowly unraveled, becoming a casualty of time and circumstance. The encounter, though brief, left an imprint on my soul, a silent exchange etched into the ever-growing story of our shared history.

As our paths diverged, I carried the weight of that moment with me, feeling the unspoken emotions settle deep within. The morning, once ordinary, had transformed into a canvas streaked with hues of bittersweet farewells. The unspoken words lingered like shadows, whispering of the complexities of love, loss, and the inevitable ache of parting ways.

In that emotional moment, the silence between us carried a weight that no words could match, imprinting itself permanently on the pages of my life. One chapter had come to an undeniable close, its final sentence written in unspoken farewells. Yet, the next chapter remained unwritten—its pages blank, filled with the uncertainty of what lay ahead, waiting to be shaped by the unknown possibilities before me.

My children, my little anchors in a sea of turmoil, emerged from their rooms, wrapped in the warmth of their favorite blankets. Spider-Man clutched in one hand, a unicorn in the other, they nestled onto their bean bags, their innocent smiles shielding them from the storm quietly brewing within our family. I greeted them with hugs and morning cheer, my voice steady, but beneath the surface, an unspoken truth lingered— one too heavy for their young hearts to bear.

In the background, my ex-wife moved through the motions of her morning routine, her presence a quiet shadow in the bathroom mirror. The physical barrier between us mirrored the emotional chasm that had grown over time—two people once bound by love, now navigating the same space as strangers.

As my children became absorbed in their morning cartoons, though in reality, a loop of nursery rhymes, I rose from my chair and joined them. Sitting beside them, I watched their eyes light up at the colorful images on the screen, their laughter filling the room with a purity I envied. But behind my quiet gaze, I faced the stark reality of my impending departure from their daily lives.

A sense of detachment settled over me, thick and consuming, like a fog I could not shake. It was not numbness, nor indifference, but a deep, sinking feeling—an emotional marsh where sorrow and helplessness blurred together, beyond my control.

Amid the rhythmic cadence of coffee sips and the soft chatter of cartoons, a dark realization settled over me like an approaching storm. This was it, the last time I would share in their morning routine, the final embrace exchanged in the quiet stillness of dawn.

I watched as my children nestled into their bean bags, their tiny forms wrapped in the warmth of familiarity, unaware of the shift about to unfold. The sight, once a simple part of daily life, now carried crushing significance. Would they remember this moment? Would they miss me in the mornings to come?

The finality of it all hung heavy in the air—an unseen weight pressing against my chest, gripping my heart, tightening around my soul. The space we shared now felt like a fragile bubble on the verge of bursting, a fleeting moment slipping through my fingers, impossible to hold onto, no matter how desperately I wished to.

As my ex-wife emerged from the bathroom, she moved

seamlessly into the kitchen, slipping into the rhythm of her morning routine. She began preparing breakfast for our children, a skill she had only embraced after they had transitioned to solid foods. It had always surprised me how, after twelve years together, she had never shown much interest in cooking until motherhood demanded it.

The kitchen, once an unfamiliar space to her, now bore the imprints of her newfound role. Yet, as I stood there, watching the sizzle of bacon and hearing the laughter of our children fill the air, it became something else—a silent battleground. Memories of shared breakfasts waged war against the present reality, forcing me to reconcile what was and what would never be again.

As the morning unfolded, our breakfast rituals became more than just routine—they became a quiet, unspoken farewell. Every movement, every clatter of dishes, every shared glance carried a weight deeper than words could express. The kitchen, a familiar stage for so many ordinary moments, now became a symphony of flavors and emotions—one final composition before the curtain fell on this chapter of our lives.

As we sat down to share the morning meal, an unspoken heaviness settled over the table, blending with the comforting aroma of breakfast. The clinking of utensils against plates echoed the bittersweet truth—this was the last time we would gather like this, the final act in a routine that had once felt so ordinary yet now held immeasurable weight.

Each bite carried a taste of longing, infused with memories of laughter, morning conversations, and the simple joy of togetherness. The warmth of the meal contrasted with the cold reality of what was slipping away. What had once been an effortless daily ritual was now a farewell in disguise—one last shared moment before the fabric of our family unraveled into something new, something unfamiliar.

The hurtful exchanges between my ex-wife and me were carefully veiled beneath a thin layer of politeness. A nod, a fleeting smile, the kind of small courtesies that carried no warmth—each gesture a quiet performance of detachment. The silence between us was louder than words, an unspoken script etched across our faces, telling a story of two people who once shared everything but now had nothing left to say.

As the clock struck 10 a.m., my ex-wife gathered the kids for a grocery run—an ordinary task now burdened with the weight of finality. I stood by the kitchen window, watching as they drove away, the taillights fading into the distance. This was it. No goodbyes, no dramatic farewells, just a quiet departure into a life I had yet to figure out.

I moved through the house with purpose, gathering what little I had left—just a few belongings, each carrying sentimental weight. The process was swift, yet each step felt drawn out, as if time itself resisted my leaving. A final scan of the rooms, my gaze lingering in the children's bedroom—where laughter, bedtime stories, and sleepy whispers once filled the air. I took a deep breath, as if trying to capture the essence of what was left behind.

Stepping out the door, I was no longer a man with a home—I was a vessel of uncertainty, waiting to be filled.

The engine of my pickup truck roared to life, its familiar hum now carrying an unfamiliar weight. I gripped the steering wheel, exhaling slowly as I faced the unknown. With $109 to my name, I pulled onto Covelo Road, Highway 162, leaving behind the remnants of a life I had once known—heading toward a future I had yet to understand.

A text from my ex-wife pierced through the turmoil, the screen glowing with a message that cut deep:

"Are you leaving? Are you even going to say goodbye to the kids? At least say goodbye to them."

My fingers hovered over the keyboard, my breath unsteadily. Every word I wanted to say felt inadequate, every response a betrayal of the truth I carried in my heart. Finally, I typed back:

"I'm not leaving. I will never leave. I'm not going to say goodbye. I will never say goodbye to my kids."

Tears welled in my eyes as I hit send, the words were both a declaration and a desperate plea against the inevitable. How do I say goodbye to what is part of my very being?

The weight of separation pressed down on my chest, suffocating in its finality. My pickup truck, once a symbol of movement and freedom, now felt like a cage—filled with the sting of unspoken words, the heavy silence of a farewell I refused to accept.

My two children, innocent, trusting souls who had known

nothing but the warmth of our shared moments, might be looking for me now, their eyes wide with confusion, their hearts struggling to understand a reality they never asked for. Were they searching for me in the familiar corners of the house? Would they call my name, expecting me to answer? The thought of their tiny faces reflecting the very pain I carried within me was almost too much to bear.

In that moment, memories crashed over me—their laughter filling the house, bedtime games that stretched long past their supposed limits, the way they clung to me in sleepy embrace after long days of adventure. How could I possibly explain what was happening? How could I make them understand that no matter the distance, my love for them was unshakable? I swallowed hard, pushing back the lump in my throat, masking my own fear as the weight of those unspoken words pressed into the walls of my pickup truck. The air inside felt thick, heavy with a love that could not be contained by physical presence alone. A family, once whole, now on the verge of breaking apart. The shared heartbeat of our bond remained—but would they always feel it? Would they always know?

To whoever finds themselves in this moment—standing at the edge of the unknown, feeling the weight of a life that is shifting beneath your feet—I WANT YOU TO KNOW THAT YOU ARE NOT ALONE.

Change, especially when it carries the ache of separation, has a way of making even the most familiar places feel foreign. The quiet mornings, once filled with certainty, now hold an unsettling stillness. The roads ahead feel unmarked, uncertain, and maybe even unbearable. But hear me when I say this: YOU WILL GET THROUGH THIS.

The love you have given, the memories you have built, the bonds that time and circumstance cannot sever—these things remain. Even when distance stretches between you and the ones you hold dearest, love does not vanish. It does not cease. It lingers in the laughter of your children, in the warmth of their embrace, in the very fabric of who you are.

I know the weight of what has been lost feels overwhelming. The unspoken words, the what-ifs, the echoes of a life that once was—all of it presses in like an unbearable storm. But storms pass. And even in the fiercest ones, the sky eventually breaks open, revealing light once more.

This chapter may feel like an ending, but it is not the end of you. You are still here. You are still capable of love, of healing, of finding purpose even in the midst of brokenness. Let the ache remind you that your heart still beats, that you still have something to give, that your presence in this world—though changed—is still profoundly important.

If today feels unbearable, take one breath at a time. If the weight of loss feels too heavy, hold on to the love that remains. And when the road ahead feels uncertain, trust that step by step, day by day, you will find your way through.

YOU ARE NOT FORGOTTEN. YOU ARE NOT ALONE. YOU ARE STRONGER THAN YOU KNOW. KEEP GOING.

Discovering His Heart

Discovering His Heart

CHAPTER 2
THE THRESHOLD OF THE UNKNOWN

Discovering His Heart

As I neared Covelo Road, a vast stretch of uncertainty unfurled before me, its scale magnified by the towering presence of Freeway 101 in the distance—a silent witness to countless journeys, each marked by its own destination. The road ahead, uncharted and unknown, stretched like an open canvas, waiting to be painted with the colors of the choices I had yet to make.

For a fleeting moment, fear threatened to creep in, whispering doubts of what lay beyond the horizon. But instead of surrendering to the weight of anxiety, an unexpected surge of confidence welled up within, a quiet but unwavering belief in my own resilience. This was not just a road; it was a threshold, an invitation to step forward into something new, something undiscovered.

Standing at the edge of Covelo Road, I made a choice—I would not let fear dictate my steps. The unknown was no longer a looming shadow but a challenge, a beckoning call to embrace what lay ahead. The winding road, disappearing into the distance, seemed to whisper its own message: Move forward. Trust the journey. The story is not over yet.

In that moment, something shifted within me—a profound recalibration of my mindset. What once felt like an overwhelming sea of uncertainty now revealed itself as a vast expanse of possibility. The unknown, instead of paralyzing me with fear, became a canvas upon which I could craft my next chapter. This was not an ending. It was an open door.

A quiet determination ignited in me, fueled by a deep-seated belief in my ability to navigate the twists and turns of life. I had faced storms before, and each one had left me stronger, more capable. The road ahead was not just a path of uncertainty, it was a proving ground for everything I had ever learned.

In the theater of my mind, I sketched a blueprint for the journey ahead—a detailed map, woven from the fabric of resilience and adaptability. Every hardship I had endured, every lesson I had internalized, and every skill I had honed over the years now came together like an intricate tapestry. This was not just about survival; it was about transformation.

As I envisioned the road ahead, I felt an undeniable connection to the power of starting over—not as a setback, but as an opportunity to rebuild everything from the ground up. I had done it before. The extensive network of professional relationships I had cultivated, the business I had helped scale to $46 million in revenue in 2019, now projected to hit $72 million by the end of 2023, stood as undeniable proof of my capabilities. This was not the end of me—it was a moment of reinvention.

I pictured a community waiting for me in the realms of CrossFit and weightlifting as I made my way back to Southern California. The gym had always been more than just a place to train—it was a sanctuary of discipline, resilience, and brotherhood. There, I would seamlessly pick up the pieces, surrounded by people who spoke the same language of grit and perseverance. With unyielding determination, I reminded myself: Everything will be fine.

I was the relentless worker, the force that never broke, the man with an unshakable work ethic. No challenge had ever stopped me before—why would this be any different?

In the mosaic of my imagination, I painted a future more refined, more powerful than anything I had built before. The love story had reached its final pages—not just at the end of a chapter, but the closing of an entire book. And now, standing at the edge of the unknown, I was ready to write a new one.

As I navigated this new chapter, filled with changes and unpredictability, I found solace and steadfastness in the presence of my two beloved children. Amidst the ebb and flow of circumstances, the unwavering bond we shared would remain my anchor, offering a sense of stability and purpose that no external force could shake. No matter what changed, they would always be my constant, my greatest reason to keep moving forward.

Yet, just as I embraced this thought, a sudden jolt shattered the harmony of my mind. A surge of unfamiliar, overwhelming emotions broke through the carefully constructed narrative of self-assurance I had built. It was as if a storm had descended without warning, clouding the clarity I had clung to. Confidence gave way to chaos, and for the first time in this journey, I felt utterly lost.

A wave of sadness and anger—directed solely at myself—rose within me, powerful and inexplicable. It was not about my ex-wife, my children, or even the divorce itself. This was something deeper, something raw and unresolved.

"What just happened?" I muttered, gripping the steering wheel, my breath uneven.

The midday sun shone brightly, yet I felt blind—as if an

unseen force had robbed me of my ability to think clearly. The road ahead twisted and turned, much like the emotions unraveling inside me. I struggled to regain composure, forcing my focus back to the drive, but my mind refused to settle.

"Why am I feeling this way? What is this unexpected sadness and anger? And why...why is it all directed at me?"

The questions echoed in my mind, but no answers came. The emotions felt like a puzzle with missing pieces, a riddle I could not solve. I blinked rapidly, trying to fight back the wetness in my eyes. It was not an allergy—I had taken my pill this morning. Yet, the tears came anyway, stubborn and relentless, defying every attempt to suppress them.

The Covelo Road stretched before me, a winding ribbon weaving through towering trees, its curves embracing the quiet mysteries of the land. Each turn held echoes of the past, a road once traveled with laughter in the backseat, my children's voices filling the spaces between the trees. This road had carried us home.

But now, as I navigated its bends alone, the memories felt heavy, almost suffocating. The same path that had once led to warmth and togetherness now served as a stark reminder of what was lost. The weight of solitude pressed against me, each mile widening the distance between my past and the unknown future ahead.

A confusing tide of emotions surged within me—grief, regret, nostalgia, and something else I could not name. The tears came without permission, slipping down my face as I gripped the wheel, trying to steady myself. I was not just driving down a familiar road, I was retracing the steps of a life that no longer existed.

The memories played in my mind like an old film reel, flickering between the golden hues of joy and the stark shadows of solitude. There was a time when this road was alive with the voices of my family, when the backseat brimmed with animated chatter, tiny hands pointing at the passing world, eyes wide with wonder.

Their heads, once nestled against car seats, would bob with excitement as they absorbed every new sight. Every turn on the road was an adventure, every mountain a towering fortress of dreams, every tree a hiding place for imaginary creatures. The car had vibrated with the harmonious symphony of toddler excitement, their laughter blending with the hum of the tires on the pavement.

The mountains, stoic and eternal, stood as silent witnesses to it all. Their peaks reached toward the sky, their shadows once playful dancers across our windshield, now looming, heavy and unmoving. The crisp scent of pine, once invigorating, now carried a weight of nostalgia, whispering secrets I could no longer decipher.

Beside me, the Eel River ran its course, winding through the landscape like a faithful companion. Its melody had once harmonized with the laughter of my children, their giggles rising above the sound of splashing water as they played along its banks. Now, the river's song felt quieter, subdued, as if mourning the absence of those carefree days.

High above, birds soared, cutting through the sky with a freedom that felt distant to me now. We used to make a game of spotting them, shouting excitedly whenever we saw a hawk or an eagle. Now, their effortless flight was a painful reminder of the distance growing between my children and me.

The road, once a conduit for shared adventures, now stretched before me as a solitary passage through the wilderness of my memories. The animals that dotted its edges—deer, squirrels, foxes, rabbits, even the occasional skunk—watched me from the safety of the brush. I used to point them out with excitement, watching my children press their faces against the glass in wonder.

Now, those same creatures stood still, their eyes reflecting something familiar, a silent, wordless understanding of the warmth of longing and the chill of loneliness.

As I drove, my mind became a cinematic reel, shifting between past and present, joy and sorrow, a fragmented mixture of emotions I could not untangle. Each mile blurred the lines between nostalgia and heartbreak, and I struggled to pinpoint the source of my tears. Was it the beauty of the landscape that triggered memories of family happiness? Or was it the unbearable contrast between then and now that crushed my chest with its weight?

The road—once a ribbon of adventure, a passage to laughter and love—now felt like a twisting maze of confusion, each curve leading me deeper into my own emotions. Darkness crept into the corners of my mind, obscuring the clarity I desperately sought. What once felt familiar now felt foreign.

What once symbolized home now mirrored my isolation.

The conflicting imagery played out like a paradox; a joyful past interwoven with a painful present. The echoes of my children's laughter still lived in the air, a ghostly symphony of memories, intertwining with the hushed sobs that now escaped my lips. I could still hear them, still feel them in the spaces between heartbeats—but they were no longer here.

The road stretched endlessly ahead, an uncertain path through a landscape of emotions, and I fought the battle between the external beauty of Covelo and the internal wreckage in my heart. What once represented connection and belonging now felt like a dividing line between what was and what is.

The mountains, the river, the birds, the deer—all silent witnesses to the unraveling of a family that once seemed unbreakable. Their presence, once comforting, now intensified the ache in my chest, a constant reminder of the fragility of happiness.

Tears continued to flow, unchecked, as I navigated the winding road. I yearned for clarity, for understanding—but all I found was longing.

In my pursuit of understanding, I gave voice to my confusion, questioning the nature of these emotions as they surged through me, unchecked. The tears—uninvited, relentless—continued their silent descent down my cheeks. I did not understand. Why now? Why here?

And then, another feeling crept in—anger. Anger at myself for surrendering to vulnerability. A voice inside me, one I had carried for years, whispered its familiar command:

"Big boys don't cry."

It urged me to be strong, to be stoic, to bury this moment of weakness before it took root. I had been fine before Covelo Road. Just fifteen minutes earlier, I was meticulously designing my future, crafting the perfect plan for my return to Southern California, envisioning success, progress, and control.

Yet something, something unseen, had shattered that fragment of perfection, replacing it with a flood of emotions I was not prepared for.

A curiosity stirred within me, an instinct I had honed over years of navigating business complexities—the natural impulse to problem-solve. Emotions, I reasoned, were no different than business challenges:

"Find the root cause. Identify the weakness. Implement a solution."

And so, I shifted my focus inward, determined to decode the essence of these emotions—to understand why they had risen so suddenly and, more importantly, how to prevent their recurrence.

The contrast between the structured future I had planned, and this unexpected unraveling became more than just an emotional disturbance; it became a test. A test of self-discovery, of resilience, of understanding the depths of my own humanity beyond logic, beyond control.

Covelo Road—once just an ordinary stretch of asphalt, a familiar pathway through the landscape of my past—had become something far greater. It now stood as a symbolic threshold, a passage not just through geography but through the hidden corridors of my own consciousness. Once a thread was woven into the fabric of our togetherness, it now bore witness to loss and transformation, holding both the warmth of shared memories and the cold truth of an uncertain future.

And so, in that impossible landscape, I drove on, chasing the elusive answer to why my tears fell so freely—why they stained Covelo Road with the salt of bittersweet memories.

To the one standing at the edge of the unknown, staring down a road that feels both vast and uncertain—I SEE YOU. I know the weight of this moment, the way the past clings to you even as the future pulls you forward. The memories, the echoes of laughter that once filled your car, the warmth of what was—it all lingers, making each step into the unknown feel heavier than the last.

But hear me: THIS IS NOT THE END. THIS IS A TURNING POINT.

Your journey has not been stripped of meaning just because the path has changed. Every hardship, every tear shed, every moment of doubt is not a sign of weakness, but of depth—of a heart that loves fiercely and a soul that refuses to be numb. The emotions that overwhelm you now are not your enemy; they are

evidence that you have lived, that you have loved, that you still care enough to feel.

You may not have all the answers yet. The road ahead may still feel uncertain. But uncertainty is not emptiness—it is potential. It is the space where transformation happens, where resilience is built, where strength is forged in the fire of experience.

Right now, it may feel as though you are unraveling, but perhaps, you are simply shedding what no longer serves you, making room for the person you are becoming. YOU ARE NOT LOST. YOU ARE IN TRANSITION. And even though this road may feel unfamiliar, you are still the one driving. You still have a say in where this journey leads.

So take this next step. Breathe deeply. Feel the ache, but do not let it chain you to the past. Instead, let it be a testament to the love and life you have experienced. And when the weight feels too heavy to bear, remember: YOU ARE STRONGER THAN YOU THINK. YOU HAVE BEEN HERE BEFORE, AND YOU HAVE RISEN.

You will rise again. Keep moving forward. The road ahead is not just un unknown—IT IS UNWRITTEN. AND YOU, MY FRIEND, STILL HOLD THE PEN.

Discovering His Heart

Discovering His Heart

CHAPTER 3
THE DETOUR INTO DARKNESS

Discovering His Heart

The road—Highway 162 to Freeway 101—stretched endlessly before me, each passing mile marked by a burden that refused to lift. It had been forty-five minutes since the storm of emotions first struck, and I had foolishly thought time would be the cure.

Yet here I was, still trapped, still drowning in the unfamiliar, uninvited turmoil that had taken hold of me. Frustration joined the growing ensemble of emotions—an unwelcome guest crashing the carefully planned trajectory of my life. The weight pressing down on my shoulders felt crushing, suffocating, eclipsing the blueprints of success and reinvention I had so meticulously constructed. Then came nervousness, creeping in like a persistent fog, obscuring the clarity I had once relied on.

As I neared the first exit into the city of Ukiah, the weight of guilt and shame cast long, suffocating shadows across my consciousness. The attack was relentless—so much so that, unable to bear it any longer, I made an impulsive decision to detour. Off the freeway. Onto Perkins Street.

I pulled into a Chevron gas station, grasping at the hope that a moment of pause, a breath of air, anything—would drown out the rising tide inside me. But the moment was fleeting. Leaving the gas station behind, I found myself steering toward Lake Mendocino, a desperate attempt to find solace in the vast stillness of the water. What was meant to be a brief stop stretched into an unexpected wandering.

Two hours later, I sat by the lake, my laptop open, fingers moving instinctively across the keyboard. And there, in the solitude of water and sky, reality and memory, longing and escape, I found myself penning an imaginary story—one that felt strangely closer to truth than I was ready to admit.

In the rhythmic cadence of my typing, I sought refuge from the storm cloud of shame and guilt that loomed over me. The keyboard became my lifeline, each keystroke made a desperate attempt to build a dam against the rising tide of emotions threatening to consume me. The story unfolded on the screen, a lake of imagination where I could release the currents of my troubled mind. Page after page, I poured my thoughts into fiction, shaping a world where control was still within my grasp. Six pages in, a realization struck me.

Without conscious intention, I had booked an Airbnb in Ukiah—an admission, perhaps, of a truth I had been unwilling to accept. The dream of heading south, returning to Southern California, starting anew—it was no longer reasonable. A gut feeling, an instinct I could not decode, had made the decision for me. A week-long stay.

The confirmation sat in my inbox, staring back at me like an undeniable truth. But rather than confront it, I continued typing. The story expanded to twelve pages, and for those hours of fictional immersion, the weight lifted. Excitement—a strange, unfamiliar excitement—replaced the suffocating guilt and shame. The world I was constructing became my sanctuary, a temporary escape from the chaos of my emotions.

But as I sat by Lake Mendocino, staring at the words on my screen, I could no longer deny what had happened. My fiction had betrayed me. The story I had written—what I had convinced myself was an escape—was instead a mirror.

A haunting reflection of my own reality, of the battle I was fighting to outrun my own pain. The characters, born from my imagination, carried the same conflicts that tore at my chest. Their emotions echoed the noise of my own shattered heart.

And yet, the relief was fleeting. As I read my own words, an unexpected revelation surfaced. The story—my refuge, my escape—had begun with an ending drenched in sorrow. A painful admission of love, tainted by the realization that I could not offer what was needed. A heartbreaking departure. A confession of my own brokenness.

The lake, once a vibrant backdrop for my attempted escape, now felt like an unrelenting mirror, mocking me with its peaceful beauty. Its surface, smooth and untroubled, denied the turbulence lurking beneath—just as I had denied my own.

I had sought comfort here, a delay from the storm raging within me. But the relief I had imagined never came. Instead, I found myself at a crossroads, torn between the story I had written and the reality I was desperate to escape. Were my words my salvation? Or my condemnation?

The contradiction gnawed at my insides, a battle between the fiction I had crafted and the truth I had avoided. Could writing truly soothe the wounds of reality? Or was it merely a reflection of them, demanding to be faced?

Frustration built within me as I closed my laptop, the weight of the decision settling on my shoulders like a heavy blanket. What had begun as a journey of escape had transformed into an unplanned quest for self-discovery. I could not outrun the shadows of guilt and shame—they clung to me, a relentless presence whispering accusations in the quiet recesses of my mind.

As I drove through the scenic landscapes surrounding the lake, heading back to Ukiah, the contrast between the external beauty and my internal turmoil was almost unbearable. The mountains, majestic and unmoved, seemed to mirror the peaks and valleys of my emotional landscape, their silent presence both comforting and cruel.

Each turn in the road brought a new revelation, a fresh wave of reflection that threatened to pull me under. My thoughts churned, restless and unrelenting, as if the very act of driving was peeling back layers I had long tried to suppress.

Seeking distraction, or perhaps relief, I decided to explore the city of Ukiah, hoping that the unfamiliar surroundings would momentarily quiet the relentless soul-searching that refused to let me go.

The town welcomed me with extraordinary streets lined with charming shops and inviting cafés, a scene so picturesque it felt like a temporary refuge from the storm inside me. I wandered, taking in the simplicity of life unfolding around me—strangers chatting over coffee, the scent of fresh bread wafting from a nearby bakery, a street musician lost in his melody.

Days turned into nights, and Ukiah became both my retreat and my prison. What was meant to be a temporary stay had transformed into a silent witness to my internal struggles. The city, with all its welcoming charm, could not shield me from the turmoil that had taken root within.

I found myself revisiting the story I had penned by the lake, combing through the words as if they held a hidden message, a revelation just beyond my grasp. What once brought me fleeting comfort now mirrored the very pain I was trying to escape. The characters, shadows of my subconscious, seemed to mock my attempts at self-deception, their struggles too close to my own.

In this self-imposed exile, I wrestled with the growing realization that true healing could not be found in the pages of a fictional tale. The lake, the story, the city, they were not the solution. They were reflections of the battle raging within me, demanding confrontation, not avoidance.

That evening, as the sun dipped below the horizon, casting long shadows over Ukiah's surrounding mountains, I found myself drawn back to Lake Mendocino once more. The water, now bathed in the colors of twilight, seemed to hold the answers I had been chasing.

My journey, with all its twists and turns, had led me back to where it began. With a heavy breath, I let go of the illusion of escape and finally embraced the vulnerability of confronting my own truth. The lake—once a sanctuary of creativity—now reflected only the turbulence within me, its once-still surface now an unsettling mirror of the storm I could no longer outrun.

I am broken; my pieces scattered across the emotional landscape of my journey. The mountain roads bore witness to my unraveling. The Chevron gas station held the fragments of my shattered resolve. Lake Mendocino cradled the birth of a story—a reflection of the chaos within me.

My body, in shock, fought against the overwhelming intensity of emotions, unsure of how to navigate the unexpected disturbance in my soul. I had never prepared for this. And yet, the lake remained still, a silent, unwavering presence, mirroring the resilience of its waters. It whispered a gentle truth: Healing is an ebb and flow. It cannot be rushed.

Standing at its edge, I felt the weight on my shoulders begin to lift. The shame and guilt, though not entirely erased, became bearable. The broken pieces of my spirit, once scattered across this journey, slowly began to find one another, weaving into quiet strength.

Lake Mendocino, with its silent wisdom, became more than a place—it became a symbol of acceptance. A reminder that in confronting my deepest wounds, I would find the strength to rebuild. One shattered piece at a time.

To the one who feels lost in the weight of their own emotions, standing at the edge of their own unraveling—I want you to know that you are not alone.

It is in moments like these, when the storm inside refuses to settle, that we often mistake our brokenness for failure. But brokenness is not the end of you. It is the beginning of something deeper, something more honest, something real. The weight you carry—the guilt, the shame, the exhaustion from trying to outrun your own emotions—does not define you. IT IS SIMPLY A CHAPTER IN THE STORY, NOT THE CONCLUSION.

Discovering His Heart

You may find yourself searching for escape, for distractions, for something to drown out the relentless noise inside. But as you have already discovered, avoidance does not heal wounds—it only prolongs their presence. The emotions that feel unbearable now are not here to destroy you; they are here to be acknowledged, to be seen, to be felt. Healing is not a sprint—it is a slow, winding journey through the terrain of your own heart.

You do not have to have all the answers today. You do not have to be "okay" right now. You only need to keep moving forward, step by step, breath by breath. The stillness of the lake, the road stretching before you, the quiet moments in between—they are not empty spaces. They are invitations. Invitations to sit with your heart, to embrace the discomfort, and to trust that even in the unknown, YOU ARE BEING SHAPED INTO SOMETHING STRONGER.

There is no shame in feeling deeply. There is no weakness in breaking apart. True strength is found in the willingness to confront the pain, to let it pass through you rather than define you. You are more than the mistakes, the regrets, the burdens you carry. YOU ARE STILL HERE. YOU ARE STILL BECOMING.

One piece at a time, you will rebuild. One day at a time, the weight will lift. And even if it does not feel like it now, there is still beauty ahead, waiting for you to step into it.

You are not alone in this. KEEP GOING.

Discovering His Heart

Discovering His Heart

CHAPTER 4
THE WEIGHT OF RETURN

On that early Sunday morning, I found myself unexpectedly drawn into the quiet sanctuary of The River of Ukiah—a decision seemingly made without my conscious recollection.

The metal chair beneath me, though unfamiliar, offered a strangely comforting embrace as I settled into its support. Around me, the calmness of the sacred space slowly filled with the soft murmur of arriving churchgoers, their presence adding a subtle hum of anticipation to the atmosphere.

In my peripheral vision, a towering figure caught my attention—standing at an impressive 6 feet 5 inches, moving with a grace that contradicted his sheer size. With each confident step, he closed the distance, his presence exuding both authority and warmth.

Stopping beside my seat, he extended his hand, his smile genuine and inviting, radiating a kindness that seemed to cut through the weight I had been carrying. His eyes, filled with sincerity, conveyed a joy that felt both foreign and oddly reassuring.

"Hi, I'm Pastor Mike. I am happy that you are here."

In that moment, I was not just another visitor in a church pew. I was seen.

As I sat in silent contemplation, the air around me felt charged with a holy expectation, wrapping me in a cocoon of stillness I hadn't known I needed. The atmosphere held a weight, a presence, as if something unseen yet undeniable was moving through the room.

When the worship songs began, I stood instinctively, following the lead of those around me. But as the lyrics unfolded, each word felt like shards of glass piercing through the walls I had so carefully built.

I opened my mouth to sing—but no sound came. Instead, a silent prayer echoed within me, wordless and raw. My voice had abandoned me, as if my soul had pressed mute on itself.

Throughout the service, my lips remained still, my voice trapped beneath the weight of emotions I could not name. The only sound I contributed to that sacred space was the quiet fall of my tears, slipping past my defenses, carrying the prayers I could not speak. I was physically present but spiritually wandering, a lone traveler in a sea of believers.

The congregation swayed with the cadence of the sermon, their spirits lifted and engaged, yet I stood there—an island of separation amid the collective flow. The pastor's words washed over me—heard but not received, present but not absorbed. The church, though warm and welcoming, felt like a distant shore, and I was a castaway, drifting in the open waters of my own thoughts, lost in the storm of my own making.

As the final song echoed through the room, I hurried toward the exit, eager to escape the anxiety tightening around my chest. I moved quietly, deliberately, slipping out unnoticed, avoiding the warmth of lingering glances, the possibility of connection.

The people were there—smiling, worshiping, alive in their faith—but between us stretched a chasm I could not cross. An emotional distance so vast that, despite the crowd, I had never felt more alone.

I drove away in silence, the hum of the engine drowned out by the questions ringing in my mind, relentless and accusing.

"Who was I to seek comfort in the arms of Yahweh when, in the Summer of 1999, I had intentionally turned my back on Him?"

The past resurfaced, a haunting vision demanding acknowledgment—a ghost that refused to be ignored. I had walked away from Him, abandoned my faith, left Him in the bays of my past.

And now? Now, in my brokenness, in my lowest place, I was daring to seek Him? To ask for refuge in the presence I had long rejected. Tears blurred the road beneath me, distorting the painted lines, turning the journey ahead into an abstract path of uncertainty. The weight of my past pressed against me; a burden I was not sure I had the right to lay at His feet.

"Why would Yahweh extend a hand to help me when I had walked away, leaving Him behind?"

In the quiet aftermath of the church service, I found myself face to face with the inconsistencies of my life—physically surrounded by a community, yet spiritually trapped in isolation, wandering through a space of self-discovery I had not been prepared to enter.

Days turned into nights, and the questions remained, escorting me like shadows, their presence inescapable. The silence that followed that Sunday morning felt louder than any worship song sung in that sacred space.

I wrestled with my faith, with the fragile thread that still connected me to Yahweh, stretched thin by choices, regrets, and the constant pull of His divine grace. And then, in the stillness of the moment, I scrutinized my surroundings—and an undeniable realization dawned upon me. I was there.

Despite everything, despite my doubts, my failures, my long departure from faith—I had found myself within the walls of a church once more. That truth alone carried a weight I could not ignore.

Amidst the turmoil within, I saw a reflection of a past self, a version of me that had once taken refuge in the presence of Yahweh, who had once found meaning and purpose in surrendering to His will. And this return—unexpected, hesitant, yet undeniable—was more than coincidence. It marked the beginning of a journey filled with questions, uncertainties, and the quiet whispers of salvation calling from a higher power.

To the one who has felt the weight of this journey, who has walked into a church feeling both drawn and distant, who has stood among believers yet felt like an outsider. I see you. More importantly, YAHWEH SEES YOU.

The questions you carry, the doubts that whisper accusations, the memories of your past that try to tell you that you do not belong—THEY DO NOT DISQUALIFY YOU. Your presence in that sacred space, even in silence, even in hesitation, is evidence of something deeper than you may realize. It is proof that Yahweh has never let go of you, that even in your wandering, He was waiting.

If you wrestle with whether you have the right to return, LET THIS BE YOUR ANSWER: YOU DO. Not because you have earned it, but because His love has never depended on your perfection. He does not turn away those who return to Him—He runs to them.

That feeling of being seen, of being drawn in despite your hesitation—that was no accident. The fact that your heart stirred, even as your mind resisted, is a sign that Yahweh is calling you back. Not with shame. Not with condemnation. But with GRACE, MERCY, AND LOVE THAT HAS NEVER WAVERED.

You may not have all the answers yet. That's okay. Keep showing up, even if your voice falters in worship. Keep seeking, even if your heart feels torn between regret and redemption. YOU ARE NOT TOO FAR GONE. YOU ARE NOT UNWORTHY. YOU ARE STILL HIS.

And if the silence after the service feels deafening, if the questions still press heavy on your chest, remember this: THE FACT THAT YOU ARE WRESTLING WITH FAITH MEANS FAITH IS STILL ALIVE IN YOU. Yahweh has not given up on you, and He never will.

So take a deep breath. You are on the path home. KEEP GOING.

Discovering His Heart

Discovering His Heart

CHAPTER 5
THE ROAD THAT CARRIED MY SORROW

The first glows of sunrise barely kissed the sky as I woke in Ukiah, the cold reality of my situation cutting through the haze of sleep. The weight of my stress-laden body pressed into me, a relentless reminder that something necessary had been left behind at my ex-wife's parents' house. The realization hit like a sledgehammer—I had to go back.

I dialed the number for a storage unit, securing a space to house the remnants of my life. Then came the call to my ex-wife—a simple conversation that carried the weight of everything we had been, and everything we would never be again. The anticipation gnawed at my inside as I braced for her response.

What unfolded next was unexpected—and, in its own way, overwhelming. Her voice, once a familiar melody, now held an unfamiliar chill. There was no hesitation, no emotion as she casually informed me that my belongings had already been removed from the shelter of her parents' barn.

No discussion. No warning. No trace of the life I had once lived within those walls. Everything I had left behind—what little remained of my existence—was now exposed to the elements, waiting for me to collect the fragments of my shattered life. The illusion of a shared history collapsed, leaving me alone with the brutal, unfiltered truth—I had been erased.

I made my way back to the scene of my separation, the silence of the drive thick with anxiety and desperation. My hands gripped the steering wheel, knuckles white, as if holding on to something that was already slipping through my fingers.

Discovering His Heart

As I approached, the scene unfolded like a dark picture—stark, unavoidable. There, on the driveway, stood my two precious kids. Their small figures were outlined against the dim glow of morning, a fragile image of innocence on the edge of a tainted truth.

Had they sensed my arrival? Or had their mother whispered the bitter truth of my departure into their unsuspecting ears?

Their eyes met mine—soft, searching, filled with a mixture of understanding and confusion. The weight of their stare sank into my soul, a silent plea for reassurance, for a fragment of normalcy in a world that had suddenly changed.

And yet, there was hope. A flicker in their eyes—a belief that this moment was just a pause, not a permanent fracture. In that instant, my heart ached under the weight of love and loss, a contradiction too vast to reconcile. Their tiny feet moved instinctively toward me, and as their arms wrapped around me, I found solace in the only place I had left—their embrace.

For one fleeting moment, the world outside ceased to exist. I was cocooned in the warmth of their affection, holding onto them as if I could freeze time, as if I could somehow protect them from the pain I knew was coming.

Hand in hand, we walked toward the barn, a silent march of shattered togetherness. Their tiny hands eagerly reached for objects that, to them, were nothing more than things—oblivious to the emotional storm spinning around us.

As we loaded my life into the back of my pickup truck, the

gravity of the moment bore down on my shoulders, pressing me into a reality I was not ready to face. This was it.

As we finished, I knelt before them, wanting to freeze this moment in time.

"I love both of you so much," I whispered, my voice betraying the turmoil within.

"I'm going to miss you so much that I won't even know what to do with myself."

And then, the lie came—a mixture of deceit and necessity, tasting bitter on my lips before the words even left them.

"Daddy is just leaving for work… this time just a little bit longer, so I can make money to buy a nice castle for you both. A prince and a princess should live in a castle."

A tale of departure and return, spun out of desperation, a castle built from words, designed to shield them from the storm. Their innocent eyes sparkled with belief, soaking in the fantasy, unaware of the cracks in the mask I wore.

I held them close. And in that embrace, the weight of my deception crushed me from within. With a heavy heart, I placed them back into the arms of their mother, their anchor in this turbulent sea of uncertainty.

And then, with nothing left to hold onto, I let go.

Driving away, the rearview mirror framed the image I never wanted to see—their tiny hands waving goodbye. The driveway stretched before me, not just as pavement, but as a path through time, winding from the house to East Lane, less than a mile away—yet an eternity in my heart.

As I approached the road, memories rushed in, unbidden, flooding my mind with the weight of every step that had ever been taken here. It was as if the asphalt itself carried the echoes of our laughter, our love, our life together.

This was not just a drive. It was the longest journey of my life—not in miles, but in the emotional expanse it covered. Every inch of road beneath my tires felt like a severed connection, a painful reminder that some distances are not measured in miles, but in the spaces that grow between hearts.

I paused, standing at the edge of the creek, and let the memories unfold upon the water like a movie—scenes flickering across the rippling surface, reflections of a past I could never reclaim.

The sunlight danced upon the gentle currents, illuminating glimpses of laughter-filled walks, tiny footprints in the mud, and the echoes of my children's voices calling out in delight. I saw us skipping rocks, their wide-eyed amazement with every ripple, their little hands reaching for mine, seeking guidance, seeking comfort. The four-wheeler's hum echoed faintly in the wind, the ghost of our past adventures still lingering in the trees.

Each moment played out like a silent film, both beautiful and unbearable, pulling me into the depths of nostalgia until I could no longer tell where the past ended, and the present began. The creek had become more than water—it was a mirror, a storyteller, a keeper of the life we had built here.

And as I stood there, watching my memories drift along the current, I realized that though time had moved forward, a part of me would always remain in the waters of that creek, forever skipping stones into the past.

As I reached the end of the driveway, where Dobie Lane and East Lane met at the horizon, I turned for one last glance.

The memories stood like silent night guards, keeping watch over the passage of time, refusing to fade. This driveway, once a lively path of shared laughter and love, now stretched before me as a quiet witness, a road that had carried the weight of my family's joy and now, its unraveling.

And in that silent farewell, I bore the weight of a thousand heart-wrenching memories, each one etched into the less-than-a-mile journey from home to the world beyond. This time, I did not fight the emotions. I surrendered. I let the tears fall freely, unchecked, unrestrained.

As I pulled onto the road to Ukiah, it became a river of sorrow, each mile carrying me farther and farther away from the only constants in my life—my children. They remained behind, standing in the wake of my fractured fairy tale.

To the one who has walked this road, who has felt the unbearable weight of parting, who has carried the silent grief of letting go—I see you. And more importantly, YAHWEH SEES YOU.

Discovering His Heart

There is no easy way to leave a place where love once flourished. There is no painless way to drive away from the ones who hold your heart. The road ahead may feel empty, hollow, stretching endlessly into an uncertain future. And in that emptiness, the memories rush in—filling the silence, breaking you open, reminding you of what once was and what can never be the same again.

But even in this heartbreak, YOU ARE NOT ALONE. Even in the moments when your chest tightens, when the ache seems too much to bear, when the tears come without permission—YOU ARE NOT FORGOTTEN. Yahweh does not turn away from broken hearts; He draws near to them. He collects every tear, He understands the weight of every step, and He walks this painful road with you.

Your love for your children is not measured by your presence alone. It is measured by the depth of your devotion, by the prayers you whisper in the quiet, by the unwavering way you hold on to hope even when the world tells you to let go. THEY MAY NOT UNDERSTAND NOW, BUT THEY WILL ONE DAY. And when they do, they will know that your love never left them—it remains steady, constant, unshaken.

You are not defined by this loss. You are not just a man driving away from his past—you are a father, a fighter, a soul who still has purpose beyond this heartbreak. This road is not the end of your story. IT IS A PAINFUL, NECESSARY TRANSITION TOWARD SOMETHING NEW. A place where healing is possible, where redemption still exists, where Yahweh is waiting to meet you in the wreckage and build something even greater.

For now, let yourself feel. Let yourself grieve. But do not let sorrow convince you that you have been abandoned. YOU ARE LOVED. YOU ARE SEEN. YOU WILL RISE AGAIN. And one day, the miles between you and your children will not feel like a chasm, but like a journey that led you back to them—stronger, wiser, and full of the grace that carried you through.

Keep going. YAHWEH IS WITH YOU.

Discovering His Heart

Discovering His Heart

CHAPTER 6
THE ROAD REMEMBERS

Discovering His Heart

As the first traces of morning painted the sky in hues of gold over Ukiah, I found solace in my quiet ritual—starting the day with a steaming cup of coffee. The rich aroma of freshly brewed beans filled the air, awakening my senses, a quiet reassurance that a new beginning was unfolding.

Seated in the peaceful stillness of my Airbnb, I found unexpected comfort in conversation with the owner—a warm soul who spoke of the town's hidden gems, its quiet charm. Amid our casual chat, he paused, offering a genuine prayer for my journey ahead—a simple, heartfelt gesture that echoed through the stillness of the morning. In that moment, it was enough.

Outside, my pickup truck waited, its back seats holding two suitcases and a backpack—silent symbols of transition, of change. The hum of the engine marked the beginning of my transformative journey, a journey guided by the warmth of morning coffee and the unexpected kindness of a stranger's prayer.

Yet, even as my divorce papers lay tucked away in the glove compartment, their presence lingered in the air like a heavy fog.

The engine rumbled to life, and I pulled away from the Airbnb, leaving behind the space that had sheltered me for a week in Ukiah. In the rearview mirror, the empty car seats stared back at me, silent and cruel reminders of the absence that now filled my world.

The weight of my decision—to leave my two precious kids with their mother—pressed down on my chest, making it hard to breathe, suffocating in its finality. The radio played softly, but no song could drown out the crashing silence that filled the car, that filled me. And so, I drove on.

Freeway 101 stretched before me like a familiar ribbon, a pathway woven with memories and emotions, unraveling mile by mile. The steady hum of tires on pavement became a heartbeat, a rhythmic echo of my own conflicted emotions.

With each passing sign, the landscape of my past intertwined with the reality of the present—every mile marker a painful reminder, every stretch of road engraved with the weight of loss. This drive was not just a route, it was a journey through the hallways of my heart.

And as the pain surfaced, I recalled the days when the back seat of my car was filled with the music of my children's laughter. They were my co-pilots, faces pressed against the glass, eyes wide with wonder, watching the world blur past.

But now, that laughter was gone. The silence was haunting, saturating the car, amplifying the aching hollowness in my chest.

Connecting to Freeway 580, I felt the shift—the highway itself seemed to mirror the twists and turns of my emotions. Every curve, every stretch of road carried me deeper into the bays of my memories, each bend a reflection of the twists in my heart.

As I pulled into a rest stop, once beacons of joy, now felt like painful pauses in the journey, the familiar spasm of loss gripped my heart. I could almost hear the echo of little footsteps of my kids running up and down the little hills with the excited shouts as they rejoiced in the freedom of open space.

The hills, once alive with their laughter, now stood as silent spectators, an eerie stillness, to the void that had taken their place. This place, once a stage for our family rituals, had become a foreign land where I now walked alone.

The road unfolded before me, and as Freeway 5 loomed ahead, a sense of inevitability settled in. This stretch of highway mirrored the widening gap between what once was and what remained.

The landscape blurred—not from speed, but from tears welling in my eyes. I longed for the simplicity of the past—when the road was just a means to a destination, not a metaphor for the unraveling of my heart.

As I merged onto Freeway 210, the hills on both sides rose in the distance, their ascent mirroring my uphill battle to reconcile the past with the present. The memories of our family drives, the shared glances as we marveled at the world together, played like old film reels in my mind. Each peak, each valley, each stretch of road held a snapshot of our history.

The rest stops on 210, once brief moments of joy, tiny pit stops for adventure—became painful markers of longing. The air still carried the echoes of laughter and whispered secrets, yet the silence that had replaced them was crushing in its intensity.

I stood alone, surrounded by the ghosts of memories, unable to escape the gravity of emotions that anchored me to everything I had lost.

Then came Freeway 15, the final leg of my heart-twisting journey. The road stretched ahead, leading to a destination I could barely define. The gas stations, the valleys, the hills, all of them became symbols of the pain that traveled with me.

With every passing mile, I was not just covering physical distance—I was navigating the widening chasm between the past and the present, desperately trying to weave my way through the web of grief.

The freeway signs flashed by, and each one marking a point of no return. The ache in my heart intensified, and for the first time, I felt as though even the road itself mourned the absence of laughter, the chaos, the love that once filled it.

Every mile carried me farther from the familiar embrace of home, and as the scenery changed, so did the rhythm of my thoughts.

The sun dipped low on the horizon, casting long shadows across the road. A symbolic sunset. Marking the end of one chapter. And the beginning of an uncharted journey.

I snuck glances at the rearview mirror, half-expecting to see their little faces looking back at me—wide-eyed, angelic, filled with the innocence of love untainted by separation. But the rear seats were empty. Their absence was a void, a hole in the fabric of my reality—one that no amount of distance could mend.

I exhaled a shaky breath, attempting to push down the

pain that clung to every thought, every memory, every breath. The questions of an uncertain future haunted me, their voices tangled in the hum of my tires against the pavement.

I reached for my sunglasses in the center console, shielding my eyes—not just from the glare of the setting sun, but from the emotional turbulence threatening to pull me under. The road signs blurred—not just from speed, but from the tears that refused to be contained.

And then, the final realization settled in like a storm cloud, darkening everything inside me. I had left my children behind, a truth that cut deeper than I could have ever imagined.

I could not help but wonder—did the road ahead hold the promise of healing? Or would it simply lead me deeper into the tangled web of grief?

As I neared the end of my journey on Freeway 15, the city lights blinked in the distance like distant stars. The road had become a bridge between the past and the present, carrying me forward whether I was ready or not.

And as I drove toward the unknown, I felt a strange sense of resignation settle over me. The pain was still there, a dull ache buried deep in the recesses of my heart—but with each passing mile, a glimmer of acceptance surfaced. An acknowledgment that life, like the Freeway, moved forward—even when the landscape was forever changed.

The exit signs approached, signaling the end of this heart-wrenching journey. The tears, though still present, were no longer a flood—but a quiet stream. I took the off-ramp, the city lights growing brighter, pulling me into a reality both unfamiliar and unavoidable.

As I parked my pickup in the quiet of the night, the hum of the engine faded, and the stillness wrapped around me. The cool night air surrounded me as I stepped out, gazing at the city lights that sparkled like distant constellations.

The journey had been raw, unforgiving, and a rollercoaster of emotions that left me vulnerable and exposed. And yet, amidst the pain, I recognized something deeper—the quiet endurance of the human spirit, the ability to suffer, to grieve, and eventually, to heal.

The road behind me stood as proof of the love that had once filled the spaces between the miles—a love that, no matter how fractured, would never be erased.

To the one who has traveled this road of loss and longing, who has felt the ache of empty car seats and the silence where laughter used to live—I want you to know that your love is not diminished by distance.

This journey you are on is not just about miles traveled; it is about the transformation happening within you. Every memory that surfaced along the highway, every tear that blurred your vision, every ache that sat heavy in your chest—these are not signs of weakness. They are reminders that YOU HAVE LOVED DEEPLY, AND THAT LOVE DOES NOT SIMPLY DISAPPEAR.

Discovering His Heart

You may feel as though you have left a part of yourself behind, that the past is slipping through your fingers with every mile. But know this: THE BOND BETWEEN YOU AND YOUR CHILDREN IS NOT MEASURED IN PROXIMITY. It is measured in the countless moments of love, in the way your heart still beats for them no matter where you are, in the prayers you whisper when no one else is listening.

The road ahead may feel uncertain. The pain may feel unbearable at times. But even now, YOU ARE MOVING FORWARD. Not away from love, but toward healing. Toward growth. Toward becoming the man your children will one day look at and see not just the heartbreak, but the strength it took to rise from it.

Let yourself grieve, but do not let grief convince you that you are alone. YOU ARE STILL A FATHER. YOU ARE STILL WORTHY OF LOVE. YOU ARE STILL ON A JOURNEY THAT HAS PURPOSE, EVEN IF YOU CANNOT SEE THE DESTINATION YET.

So keep going. Keep believing that, even on the loneliest stretches of road, YAHWEH IS WITH YOU. Keep trusting that though this season is painful, it is not the end of your story. YOU WILL FIND YOUR WAY. You will heal. And one day, the miles that feel like separation will become the very path that leads you back to wholeness.

YOU ARE NOT FORGOTTEN. YOU ARE NOT FORSAKEN. KEEP DRIVING, KEEP HOPING—THERE IS STILL LIGHT AHEAD.

Discovering His Heart

Discovering His Heart

CHAPTER 7
LAUGHTER, LOVE, AND SILENT GOODBYES

Sixteen hours after embarking on this journey, I finally reached Eastvale, the city we had once envisioned as the foundation for raising our two precious children. But life, ever unpredictable, had its own script to follow.

The moment of arrival, which should have carried a sense of relief, instead brought a stark realization, I had no designated place to stay. The weight of uncertainty settled in. Like a sudden gust of wind stripping away illusions of stability, the reality of my situation unfolded before me—raw and unfiltered.

Yet, in that moment of vulnerability, family stepped in. With open hearts and unwavering generosity, my siblings extended their home to me, becoming a beacon of warmth and refuge amid the chaos.

Their hospitality was more than just an offer of shelter, it was a reminder of the unshakable strength of familial bonds. In a moment where circumstances seemed to hang in fragile balance, their kindness became an anchor, grounding me in the midst of uncertainty.

Their home, once just a place of familiarity, now stood as a sanctuary, a space where adversity transformed into an opportunity for shared strength and resilience. And in that, I was reminded: Even in life's unexpected detours, the open arms of loved ones can turn hardship into a foundation for healing.

The first week unfolded like a delicate dance—shared spaces, shared moments, shared silences. Laughter echoed through the walls, wrapping around us like a long-lost embrace, filling the spaces where time had once created distance. We caught up on life, exchanging stories that bridged the years apart, weaving the past into the present with each reminiscence and cherished memory.

Yet, as days melted into nights, my siblings began to notice the silent earthquakes beneath my smiles, the subtle tremors of pain hiding in the corners of my weary expression. They saw me. And without words, they became my steady anchors, sensing the unspoken grief that clung to me like an invisible weight.

Late at night, while the world outside slept, my sister sat beside me—a quiet guardian in the slow glow of our shared sanctuary. With patience and care, she helped me unwrap the layers of my trauma, as if peeling away the fragile paper of a long-neglected gift.

Each revelation met with nothing but warmth. Her words—a soft refuge against the storm in my heart—whispered promises of a tomorrow untouched by the shadows of my past.

Meanwhile, my brother became the keeper of laughter. With jokes that disarmed the darkness and stories crafted to chase away ghosts, he reminded me that joy was still within reach. In the warmth of his presence, I found fleeting moments of relief—brief reprieves from the haunting echoes of loss.

For a while, I let myself sink into the comfort of their love, allowing the stitches of their kindness to begin mending the unraveling fabric of my soul. But the temporary nature of my stay became inevitable—a simple pause in the rhythm of their everyday lives.

As the second week unfolded, the shadow of my impending departure grew longer, stretching over our time together. The laughter, once bright and unburdened, now carried an undertone of farewell—a silent acknowledgment of the goodbye that loomed ahead.

Southern California sun cast its golden glow over my temporary refuge at my sister and brother's home, an unexpected heaviness settled within me. The promise of a fresh start, which had once fueled my journey south, now felt less like an adventure and more like an overwhelming challenge.

Even in the warmth of family love and support, I found myself grappling with an emptiness so vast that I did not know where to begin.

Each morning greeted me like a blank canvas, yet the brush of motivation eluded me. The desire to rebuild was there, but navigating uncharted territory without a clear path felt paralyzed. Days melted into a fog of uncertainty, as I stared at the metaphorical canvas of my life, longing to paint a brighter picture but unsure of where to place the first stroke.

Even the encouraging conversations with my siblings, though filled with love and reassurance, could not chase away the shadows that clung to my thoughts. The weight of expectation—both self-imposed and perceived—scrambled the landscape of my ambitions, leaving me feeling adrift in a sea of doubt.

In the vastness of Southern California, I felt small, overwhelmed by the magnitude of the task ahead. It was not just about physical relocation, it was about reshaping the outlines of my life, about finding purpose in the void, about writing a new narrative for myself in a place that no longer felt like home.

Even with the ocean's rhythmic whispers and the palm trees swaying in quiet reassurance, the sense of uncertainty lingered. It was not a lack of love or gratitude that weighed me down, it was the realization that my internal compass had lost its direction.

Grateful for the warmth and generosity of my siblings, I knew my time under their roof was a brief but necessary chapter.

The Southern California sun illuminated not just the palm-lined streets, but also the road that led me back north—back to my true anchors—my children, waiting for me in Northern California.

With heartfelt goodbye, I embarked on the journey back up the coast, the highway stretching out before me like a ribbon, connecting the scattered chapters of my life.

And as I crossed back into Northern California, the ache of separation faded, replaced by something stronger, the undeniable eagerness to reunite with my children, the one constant in my ever-changing story.

To the one who has felt lost in transition, who has stood at the crossroads of uncertainty, searching for a sense of home in a place that no longer feels familiar—I see you. AND MORE

IMPORTANTLY, YAHWEH SEES YOU.

You are not alone in the ache of starting over, in the weight of expectations that press down like an invisible burden. It is okay to feel overwhelmed, to wake up with a blank canvas and not know where to place the first stroke. Change, especially one born from loss, is never easy. But even in the fog of uncertainty, you are still moving forward, even when it doesn't feel like it.

Lean into the love that surrounds you, even if only for a season. Let the kindness of family, the unexpected moments of laughter, and the quiet companionship in your sorrow remind you that YOU ARE NOT FORGOTTEN. The temporary refuge you found was not just a pause—it was a gift, a reminder that even in your brokenness, you are still deeply loved.

And when the time comes to step into the unknown, DO NOT FEAR. The road ahead may seem daunting, but it is leading you somewhere meaningful. Your heart knows where it belongs, and even when doubt clouds your vision, your love for your children remains the unwavering guidepost lighting the way.

You are not lost. You are in transition. You are becoming. AND STEP BY STEP, YOU WILL FIND YOUR WAY. Keep going—YOU ARE NOT ALONE IN THIS JOURNEY.

Discovering His Heart

Discovering His Heart

CHAPTER 8
THE PROMISE THAT NEVER BREAKS

It was hard—impossibly hard—placing them down and saying goodbye. The echoes of my children's voices followed me, their innocent inquiries piercing the fabric of my soul like a haunting melody.

"Daddy, are you coming back?"

Their words, filled with hope and anticipation, reverberated within the confined space of my pickup truck, turning it into a chamber of heartaches, a soundtrack to my internal struggle. Each time I had to drive away, I fought an invisible war—one between my duty to rebuild and my desperate longing to stay.

As I stood still in silence, their heartfelt questions lingered, refusing to fade, a tender, yet agonizing reminder of the emotional tug-of-war that defined my every departure.

What was once just a pickup truck, a simple means of getting from one place to another, had transformed into a vessel of shared sentiments. It carried the weight of their expectations, the burden of my longing, and the inescapable sorrow of every goodbye.

Their innocent voices traveled with me on every journey, a poignant reminder that separation was not just my burden to bear—it was theirs, too.

And in those moments of quiet solitude, their words became more than echoes—they were a powerful thread, tying me to the depths of parental love. A love that demanded sacrifice. A love that fueled my pursuit of creating a future worthy of the moments I had to miss. A love that refused to let distance define our bond.

My rearview mirror framed their small figures, tiny hands waving goodbye with a trust so pure, so unwavering, that it was both heartwarming and heartbreaking.

As I navigated the familiar route away from their world, their voices lingered, painting an emotional landscape that mirrored the conflict tearing into the fabric of my being.

In those moments, I questioned everything, every choice, every step, every decision that had led to these painful separations. The promises I had made to them, once simple commitments of a father's love, now weighed heavily on my conscience.

"Daddy, promise that you are coming back."

Their innocence was a double-edged sword, slicing through my soul, exposing the fragility of the world I had built for them.

As I drove further away, the rearview mirror transformed into a portal to a parallel universe, one where my children remained frozen in time, forever waving, forever waiting.

The rhythmic hum of the tires became the background to the battle unfolding in my mind—How did I arrive here? How had the promises I made to my children become entangled with the expenses demanded by circumstance?

This struggle was not just physical, it was a war waged in the depths of my emotions. A battle between responsibility and the ruthless burn of separation.

My rearview mirror—an ordinary object—became something more. It became a metaphor for introspection, a reflective surface holding more than just the image of my departing children. It reflected me, the father caught in the crossfire of love and duty, longing and necessity. The weight of responsibility, like an anchor, pulled me in two directions, towards the stability I sought to build for them, and towards the bonds I feared were slipping through my fingers.

In the silence of my pickup truck, memories unfolded like a collage—pieces of bedtime stories, echoes of shared laughter, and tearful embraces. Each moment was a tender reminder of the fleeting nature of childhood, a temporary season that demanded a delicate balance between presence and absence.

The rearview mirror, with its frozen snapshots of departure, framed the irony of my existence, a father physically absent, yet emotionally bound.

As the miles accumulated, so did the weight of responsibility.

"Daddy, are you coming back?"

Their words echoed louder, reverberating within the confined space of my truck, becoming more than just a question, it was a plea, a desperate call for assurance, for security, for strength in a world that, to them, felt increasingly fragile. They were not just asking if I would return; they were asking if I was still theirs. If I was still home.

Discovering His Heart

The passing scenery outside my window became a visual metaphor for time slipping away. The landscapes changed, the world moved forward, but my struggle remained constant—an unshakable companion. I wrestled with the dual identity of being both provider and absentee father, a contradiction that challenged the very essence of what it meant to be a parent.

And with every turn of the wheel, I fought the aching truth that love, no matter how deep, could not rewrite time. But maybe—just maybe—it could still shape the future.

The rearview mirror, once just a reflective surface, had become a witness to the passage of time. It captured not only the faces of my children but also the subtle, heartbreaking shifts in their expressions.

What was once pure excitement in their wave's goodbye had slowly faded, giving way to something quieter, something heavier, a quiet acceptance. A transformation that mirrored the gradual realization in their young hearts—that Daddy's departures were not just temporary; they were a pattern, a recurring theme woven into the fabric of their childhood.

The divide between my external composure and internal turmoil felt suffocating inside the walls of my truck. The rearview mirror, once a passive observer, now reflected back at me—the weary eyes, the furrowed brow, the quiet war of a father facing the aftermath of yet another goodbye.

The road, seemingly linear, unraveled before me as something more, a narrative of sacrifice, love, and the invincible spirit of parenthood. And as I continued to drive, a realization settled in. This struggle was not mine alone. It was a shared experience, a universal ache carried by countless parents, all trying to balance the delicate act of supporting their children while being physically present.

The road became a collective journey, and in its silent spaces between heartbeats, I knew I was not alone in hearing the echoes of "Daddy, are you coming back?"

Every departure became a brushstroke on the canvas of their memories, a mosaic that would shape their understanding of love, commitment, and sacrifice.

And though the struggle was hard, gut-wrenching, and unforgiving, it held the power to shape them—not into children burdened by loss, but into resilient, understanding souls, capable of weathering life's uncertainties.

On every mile that I traveled, every ache endured, was part of something greater, a foundation being built, a safety net being woven, a future being secured.

The echoes of "Daddy, promise that you are coming back" would one day be replaced by the warmth of reunions, the stability of shared moments, and the unwavering truth that I had always, always come back.

The road ahead, with its endless twists and turns, held more than just challenges. It held the promise of homecomings that would one day reshape the story we were writing together. Each mile, though heavy with longing, carried the quiet assurance that every departure also led to a return. And so, with each passing mile, I held onto one unshakable hope. That one day, the rearview mirror would no longer reflect goodbyes. But instead, a window to the joyous reunions that awaited on the horizon.

To the one who has felt the weight of every goodbye, who has fought the battle between responsibility and the ache of absence—you are not alone.

I know how much it hurts to watch their tiny hands wave in the rearview mirror, to hear the echo of their voices asking if you'll come back, to carry the burden of building a future while longing to stay in their present. THE ROAD FEELS ENDLESS, THE MILES HEAVY, THE SACRIFICE UNBEARABLE. But hear this: YOUR LOVE IS NOT MEASURED BY PROXIMITY.

Even in the distance, you are shaping them. Your love, your devotion, your unwavering commitment to return—it all plants seeds of resilience in their hearts. THEY MAY NOT FULLY UNDERSTAND NOW, BUT ONE DAY, THEY WILL. One day, they will see the depth of your sacrifice and know that every mile travel was not away from them, but for them.

The ache of separation is real, but SO IS THE PROMISE OF REUNION. Every road that takes you away, also leads you back. EVERY TEAR SHED IN LONGING IS A TESTAMENT TO A LOVE THAT REFUSES TO BREAK. You are not forgotten. Your love is not unseen. Your presence, even in absence, is felt in every promise kept, in every moment you return, in every unwavering assurance that you are still, and will always be, their home.

Discovering His Heart

So take heart. THE ROAD AHEAD IS NOT JUST ABOUT DEPARTURE—IT IS ABOUT THE JOURNEY THAT LEADS BACK TO THEM. Keep driving, keep believing, keep holding onto hope. ONE DAY, THE REARVIEW MIRROR WILL NO LONGER HOLD GOODBYES, BUT THE REFLECTION OF HOMECOMINGS THAT MAKE IT ALL WORTH IT.

Discovering His Heart

Discovering His Heart

# CHAPTER 9
MONUMENTS OF WHAT ONCE WAS

Discovering His Heart

In the heart of Eastvale, where the city whispers its stories through every street corner, within the walls of its restaurants, and on the benches of its parks, there exists a tapestry woven with threads of memories.

Memories of a time when laughter echoed through the houses, when music wove itself into the air, and when the city stood as a silent witness to the tender moments shared by my family.

Every element of this city, once a backdrop to unfiltered joy, now stands as a tear-streaked testament to the passage of time. The streets, the restaurants, the familiar park benches, they were once simply places. Now, they are monuments.

Each one bearing silent witness to the ebbs and flows of my life—to the love that once thrived in the daylight and now lingers in the shadows of pain.

The city, once a living canvas painted in the colors of family and warmth, now tells a different story. One of love that flourished, of joy that overflowed, and of the haunting ache left behind when time refused to stand still.

The city streets, once alive with the rhythm of my family's footsteps, now whisper ghostly echoes of what used to be. Every intersection holds the weight of decisions made, paths taken, and the irreversible journey that led to a fractured home.

As I walked through these familiar avenues, the fronts of the houses reflect more than just architecture—they mirror the hidden fractures within, their walls holding onto the unspoken truths of a family now torn apart.

The restaurant where family dinners once unfolded, now a haunting scene of empty chairs and unsaid words. The scent of familiar dishes mingles, and the waitstaff, now unknowingly serve the echoes of a love that faded.

The trees lining the streets, once guardians of my children's laughter and our stolen moments of peace, now stand stoic and unmoving. Their branches reach out, as if longing to bridge the emotional gaps left behind. The leaves whisper in the wind, carrying memories of shared stories and dreams—now distant echoes swirling among the rustling branches.

The music that once scored on our family road trips, our lazy Sunday afternoons, our simplest joys, now plays a different tune. Each note, once a source of comfort, now resonates with the pain of separation, each melody a delicate but relentless reminder of a love that has become nothing more than a distant echo.

The park, once a sanctuary of innocence and laughter, now stands as a testament to the fragility of happiness. The park benches, once a place of shared solitude, of whispered dreams, of quiet companionship, now bear the crushing weight of loneliness.

And in the silence of these streets, I realize that the city itself has become a memorial to a life I can no longer call my own.

Amidst the echoes of my fractured past, a subtle transformation begins to unfold—a whisper of hope stirring in the quiet chambers of my heart.

As I walk the familiar streets of Eastvale, I sense an unseen hand guiding me, gently steering me away from the places that threaten to unravel the fragile threads of my healing. I avoid the restaurant once filled with shared laughter, the street corners that bore witness to disagreements, the houses that held the silence of unspoken words.

In this avoidance, there is acknowledgment—a silent prayer rising within me, asking for strength to move forward, to leave behind the shadows of my past.

The trees, standing tall with their quiet wisdom, become more than landmarks, they become symbols of resilience and grace. No longer haunted by the memories they hold, I find relief beneath their branches, seeking refuge in the shade they provide. The swishing leaves whisper a truth I had once struggled to hear. That like the changing seasons, there is a divine order to life. And with it, the promise of renewal.

The music, once a source of pain, now carries a different kind of melody—one of gratitude and acceptance. I choose songs that uplift rather than remind, and in doing so, feel a shift within me. Music becomes a bridge, leading me toward a higher understanding, reminding me that even in the conflicts of life, greater harmony is at play.

The park, once avoided for fear of encountering the echoes of family happiness, now becomes a sacred ground for personal reflection. As I walk its paths, my heart opens to the possibility of new beginnings, and I sense His presence in the whispers of the wind, in the sunlight breaking through the clouds.

The park benches, once symbols of loneliness, now serve as seats of sacred thought—places where I can pause, breathe, and embrace the quiet work of healing.

And in all of this, I realize that Yahweh's presence was never absent, only waiting for me to look up, to listen, and to trust.

In these conscious choices to avoid triggers, I recognize His hand at work, gently guiding me away from the painful pathways of the past.

The city itself, once a haunting maze of memories, begins to transform into a canvas, where the Divine Artist paints strokes of healing and redemption. Every step away from the old echoes becomes a step toward the promise of a brighter future.

Through prayer and reflection, I find a refuge within myself, a sacred space where His grace begins to mend my broken pieces. The struggles that once felt impossible lose their grip, and in the depths of my vulnerability, a newfound strength emerges. With each prayer, each intentional step forward, I am reminded that Yahweh is not only a distant force, but a present guide, walking with me toward healing and peace.

In the evolving story of Eastvale, the city itself becomes a symbol—not just of pain, but of resilience. A reminder that His plan unfolds in ways I never expected.

To the one who walks through streets lined with memories, where every familiar place whisper echoes of what once was—I

see you. And YAHWEH SEES YOU.

I know how heavy it feels to move through a world that used to be filled with laughter and warmth, only to now feel like a museum of what was lost. I know how it stings when a song, a park bench, or even the scent of a familiar place reopens wounds you thought had begun to heal. But hear me—THIS IS NOT WHERE YOUR STORY ENDS.

The pain may be real, but so is the transformation. The past may have shaped you, but it does not own you. YOU ARE NOT TRAPPED IN MEMORIES; YOU ARE BEING LED INTO HEALING. Yahweh does not leave you wandering through the ruins of yesterday—He is gently guiding you toward something new, something whole, something redeemed.

The same streets that remind you of loss will one day be paths of restoration. The places that now feel haunted will become markers of how far you have come. YOUR HEART WILL NOT ALWAYS ACHE LIKE THIS. The love you have lost is not gone—it has simply changed form, woven into the depths of who you are, carried forward into a future where peace is waiting for you.

And as you continue walking, even when the weight feels unbearable, remember this: YAHWEH HAS ALREADY GONE AHEAD OF YOU. He is painting something new on the canvas of your life. Even if you can't see it yet, trust that the brushstrokes of healing are already in motion.

You are not just surviving—you are being remade. ONE STEP AT A TIME, ONE PRAYER AT A TIME, ONE

BREATH AT A TIME. Keep moving forward, knowing that HIS PRESENCE IS WITH YOU IN EVERY PLACE, IN EVERY MEMORY, AND IN EVERY NEW BEGINNING.

CHAPTER 10
A LOVE THAT HAD BEEN WAITING

Discovering His Heart

On Easter Sunday morning, I found myself standing amidst the vibrant tones of spring, greeted by an unexpected invitation—one that felt like an olive branch of support. It was Robin and Jodi, reaching out through text, urging me to join them for church.

For a moment, my heart hesitated—weighed down by the relentless pain that had woven itself into the very fabric of my days and nights. But something within me stirred—a whisper of hope, a longing for even the smallest reprieve from the ache that had become an unwelcome companion. I accepted the invitation.

The thought of stepping into the sacred atmosphere of the church felt like a possibility for renewal, a glimmer of something beyond the weight of my suffering. Somewhere within the walls of that sanctuary, there might be a flicker of light strong enough to pierce through my darkness. That for even a moment, I might find relief in the presence of something greater than my pain.

As I stepped into the church, the air carried peaceful energy, a stillness that felt both foreign and familiar. Sunlight filtered through stained glass windows, casting a kaleidoscope of colors onto the pews—an unintentional work of art, painting the sacred space with a soft glow of divine welcome.

Robin and Jodi greeted me with warm smiles and genuine hugs, their enthusiasm lightening the weight of my condition. Together, we walked into an unassuming sanctuary, a place that would soon become the backdrop for a profound encounter.

As the service unfolded, its rhythm was gentle yet powerful, like a tide carrying me toward something greater than myself. Each note of the worship songs was stirring something deep within me—something long buried beneath my pain. The voices of the congregation rose and fell like a collective heartbeat, filling the air with praise, surrender, and longing.

And as the lyrics of devotion washed over me, I felt an undeniable shift in the atmosphere. It was as if the music itself became a bridge, stretching between the earth and the divine, pulling me into its current. The songs—familiar yet charged with newfound significance—carried me to a place of vulnerability I had long resisted.

And then, in that sacred space, I felt Him. Not as a distant force, but as an undeniable presence. An assurance that I was not alone and that a love far greater than human understanding was reaching out to me. A love that had been there all along, waiting for me to notice.

The words spoken felt as if they were crafted specifically for me—tailored to reach the deepest chambers of my heart. It was as though the pastor, guided by an unseen hand, unraveled the intricacies of my doubts and fears, peeling back the layers of pain I had hidden for so long. Each sentence pressed gently yet firmly against the raw nerves of my soul, resonating with a truth that transcended the walls of the church.

The message was one of redemption, a love that surpassed all understanding, reaching even the most broken places. The story of resurrection unfolded before me, not as a distant theological concept, but as a living, breathing testament to the promise of renewal.

And in that moment, I felt His embrace, an affirmation that I was not abandoned, that healing was not beyond reach. Yet, the tears continued to fall, a silent testimony to the emotional journey unfolding within me. Each tear was a release, a shedding of the weight I had carried far too long.

Beside me, Robin and Jodi became more than friends—they became conduits of His grace. Their presence, their unwavering support, was a tangible manifestation of the divine love that had orchestrated this moment. I found comfort not just in the spoken words, but in the unspoken language of shared glances and quiet understanding.

The pain I had tucked away finally found its voice. It echoed in the resonance of the hymns, in the melancholy notes of the piano, in the silent prayers whispered all around me. I felt an inexplicable connection to the shared vulnerability of the worshippers around me.

My tears flowed unbidden, carrying away fragments of pain that had silently consumed me. And for the first time, I did not fight them. I allowed myself the freedom to release the weight that words could never fully convey. My tears became an offering, an emotional surrender to Yahweh, to the healing I had resisted, to the grace that had always been waiting.

The grace I had been searching for was not some abstract concept—it was here, in this very moment. It was in my tears, in the hands on my shoulders, in the quiet empathy of those surrounding me. For the first time, I saw that grace was not reserved for the worthy, but for the willing.

I sat in stillness, raw yet whole. Kind eyes met mine, offering silent understanding, speaking a language deeper than words. There were no perfect sentences that could explain what had just happened. Because this moment was not meant to be explained, it was meant to be experienced. It was a communion—a silent, holy exchange between Yahweh and the depths of my soul.

Robin, Jodi, and Marina wrapped me in long, knowing hugs—their presence a balm to my wounded spirit. They spoke few words, yet their embrace spoke volumes, offering an empathy that transcended language itself. And in that quiet exchange, I realized something profound. Healing does not always begin with answers. Sometimes, it begins with shared tears. With compassionate hearts willing to hold space for the brokenness of another. And in that space, Yahweh was already at work, rewriting my story.

As I drove home, the sun sinking into the horizon, I carried with me the echoes of Easter Sunday—not just in my mind, but deep within my soul. The emotional weight of the church service still lingered, but it no longer felt like a burden.

My tears, once symbols of sorrow, had transformed. Now, they were sacred droplets of release, of acceptance. It was the beginning of something profound—a journey toward true healing. The tears, now dried, had paved the way for a new understanding.

A realization that Yahweh's love was not confined to the

walls of a church or the rituals of religion. It was a force greater than doctrine—one that touched the deepest, rawest parts of our humanity.

The drive that began with uncertainty ended in gratitude. Gratitude for the divine orchestration of that day, for the unexpected encounters, the silent embraces, and the unshakable presence of Yahweh guiding me forward.

The church became more than a Sunday refuge, it became a sanctuary woven into my daily life. I attended men's Bible study groups, engaged in heartfelt conversations, and discovered that healing was not a linear path. It moved like a river, sometimes calm, sometimes turbulent, but always shaping the landscape of my emotions in ways I could not yet comprehend.

My pain did not vanish overnight, but with each passing day, its sharp edges began to soften. The tears that once carried despair began to carry resilience. They became like rain nurturing the soil, fostering growth, strength, and a new kind of understanding.

In the heart of my vulnerability, I found a hidden power, a strength that was not in suppressing emotions but in embracing them. My tears became my language, a way of communicating what words could never fully express.

And in the company of those who truly listened, who truly saw me, I realized that healing was not about erasing the past, it was about transforming it. Turning it into wisdom, into compassion, and into something beautiful. And that, I knew, was where Yahweh had been leading me all along.

As I stand on the threshold of a new chapter, I carry with me the lessons learned in that church. My tears, once seen as symbols of pain, now stand as monuments of strength found in vulnerability. A reminder that even in the darkest tunnels, there is a dim light waiting to guide me toward healing and transformation.

To the one who has carried the weight of pain for far too long, who has hesitated at the threshold of healing, unsure if they are worthy of grace—THIS IS FOR YOU.

I know the battle between longing for peace and fearing the surrender it requires. I know what it is to sit in the sacred tension of worship, feeling both seen and undone. I know what it is to fight back tears, only to realize that they were never a sign of weakness—but an offering, a bridge to the heart of Yahweh.

YOU ARE NOT ALONE IN THIS JOURNEY. The pain you have carried, the questions you have wrestled with, the moments of doubt that made you wonder if you had wandered too far—NONE OF IT HAS DISQUALIFIED YOU FROM HIS LOVE. In fact, He has been waiting, not with condemnation, but with open arms, ready to welcome you into something deeper than you've ever known.

Healing does not always come in a single moment. Sometimes, it comes in the steady rhythm of surrender—the kind that happens when you allow yourself to feel, to weep, to be embraced by those who see you, who hold space for your pain, who remind you that GRACE IS NOT FOR THE PERFECT, BUT FOR THE WILLING.

Let your tears be a testament, not to your brokenness, but to the courage it takes to begin again. Let this moment be the start of something new—not an erasure of your past, but a transformation of it. Yahweh is not just in the church; He is in the whispers of comfort, in the hands that held you, in the presence that wrapped around you when words failed. HE HAS ALWAYS BEEN WITH YOU.

So take a deep breath. You are not beyond redemption. You are not too far gone. You are seen, you are loved, and you are still being written into a story far greater than you could imagine.

KEEP MOVING FORWARD. HIS GRACE IS LEADING YOU HOME.

Discovering His Heart

Discovering His Heart

CHAPTER 11
THE QUESTION THAT COULD HAVE SAVED ME

Within the unnerving silence of my phone, I found myself confronting a profound sense of digital loneliness. The absence of the usual hum of notifications, once a reassuring rhythm of personal connections, now felt like an aching void—a silence that cast shadows over the once-vibrant device in my hands. The quiet was not just stillness, it carried with it an almost tangible emptiness, amplifying the loneliness that had already settled deep within me. It was a stark departure from the usual symphony of messages and calls that once offered warmth, familiarity, and a sense of belonging.

Now, in this frightening calm, only messages tied to business transactions dared to break the stillness. But they did not fill the void. They only highlighted the contrast. Instead of the warmth of personal exchanges, my phone had become a mere conduit for impersonal dealings. The pulse of human connection had been replaced by the sterile, emotionless hum of transactions, leaving me grappling with the stark contrast between what I craved and what I received. In the cold glow of the screen, I saw not just a device but a mirror reflecting the distance between me and the world I once knew.

As I navigated through the muted hallways of my phone, the absence of personal inquiries echoed louder than any notification ever could. No friends. No family. No simple, "How are you doing?" Just silence. A stark reminder that the world had become a place where personal exchanges were overshadowed by the relentless pursuit of productivity.

My phone—once alive with laughter, shared moments, and heartfelt conversations, now stood as a silent witness to the changing landscape of my human connection. Notifications still appeared, but they carried no warmth, only business updates, invoices, and reminders that filled the screen while leaving the spaces for personal connection empty.

In a world wired for constant connectivity, I had never felt so disconnected. The quietness of my phone painted a painful contrast, lost in the shuffle of efficiency, deadlines, and professional roles. I scrolled through transactional messages, each one a pixel in the larger image of a busy life. Yet nowhere in that digital landscape was there room for a simple, "How are you?"

The absence of such words raised painful questions. Had friendship, family, and community shifted into something conditional, something secondary to busyness?

I found myself on a lonely path, a solitary journey cutting through the very fabric of my being. The pain I bore was not just physical, it ran deep. It echoed in the hollow chambers of my soul, where silence sat like an unwelcome guest. But what stung most was not just the silence itself. It was the glaring absence of those I had once believed would be there. And in that unanswered quiet, I was left to wonder. Had I been forgotten, or had the world simply stopped asking?

During this journey of difficulty, I discovered a bitter truth. Acquaintances did not always breed companionship. The substantial network of connections I once believed in turned out to be fragile threads, easily unraveling in the face of hardship.

As I wrestled with my challenges, I looked around, hoping

for a lifeline, a comforting touch, or even a single uplifting word. Yet, the silence roared louder than any words ever could. A deafening emptiness that made me realize, the multitude of faces I encountered daily were simply watchers to the production of my shadow. Passive observers who never truly recognized the subtle tones of my struggle.

What intensified the pain was not just the silence itself, it was the harsh knowledge that I had invested in relationships, believing them to be reciprocal bonds built upon shared experiences. Yet, when the storm clouds gathered overhead, and the cyclone of hardship erupted, I found myself standing alone, a solitary figure, battling against the elements, while those I once called friends stood in the distance, watching, but never stepping forward.

The quiet was frightening—not just because of its stillness, but because of the void it created. The absence of familiar vibrations, of once-constant personal connections, amplified the harsh loneliness that had settled in my soul. The digital space, once alive with messages, notifications, and shared laughter, now felt eerily silent. It was as if my contacts had retreated into the shadows, leaving me to wander the echoing hallways of my own mind, searching for signs of familiarity.

I yearned for someone to reach out, to check on me, to ask if I was okay, to remind me that I still mattered. But the weight of anticipation grew heavier, pressing down on me with each passing moment. The silence, once unsettling, now felt like an unspoken confirmation of my worst fears. That I was alone, present, but unseen.

In a desperate bid for connection, I turned to the lifeline of social media, a place where the world never sleeps, where voices are always speaking, and where I hoped, for once, someone would listen. My fingertips danced across the screen, crafting messages that were really just silent pleas, waiting for someone to bridge the growing gap.

Instagram became my canvas—a space where I spilled fragments of my soul into posts, stories, and reels. In the captions of my posts, I carefully wove threads of vulnerability, hoping that someone, somewhere, would decode the silent cries for companionship. I shared the highs and lows, the ordinary and the deep. Each one laid bare in the digital theater of my Instagram feed. Each post was a lifeline, cast into the vast ocean of social media, a beacon of connection, desperately seeking a response.

My Instagram stories became visual diaries, capturing fleeting moments of my day, hoping that someone might recognize the subtle nuances of my emotions. I shared: laughter, hoping someone would laugh with me. Quiet moments of reflection, hoping someone would see beyond the surface. Shadows of loneliness, that danced in the corners of my eyes. Each frame carried the weight of unspoken words, a silent message carved in pixels and captions.

Days turned into nights. My digital cries for connection echoed into the vastness of the internet. But the response remained vague. I struggled with questions that lingered like shadows: Did my contacts see my posts? Did they scroll past, indifferent to the silent plea embedded in each image and caption? Or had the algorithm consigned my digital cries to the forgotten corners of the virtual world?

The loneliness persisted, weaving itself into a tapestry of anticipation, vulnerability, and unanswered yearning. The digital space, once a source of connection, now mirrored the isolation that had crept into my physical world. The glow of the screen, once a beacon of hope, now cast a harsh light on the void between me and the people I once called my own.

As I continued to wait, the silence became my companion, a confusing yet familiar presence, wrapping itself around me like an unwelcome shadow. I wrestled with the impossibility of being hyper-connected in the digital world, yet still profoundly alone.

The yearning for human connection, amplified by the absence of response, created a symphony of solitude that played on an endless loop. The superficiality of likes and follows became painfully clear. In a world that promises constant connection yet delivers only silence.

Were these friendships built on solid ground, or were they fragile bonds, destined to crumble at the first shake of difficulty? The pain of abandonment wounded my spirit, leaving scars that went beyond the physical, scars that etched themselves deep into my soul. The absence of a comforting presence during my darkest hours engraved an emotional story of helplessness, a story that taught me a painful truth:

The true measure of friendship is not found in the shared laughter, but in the willingness to stand together when the world crumbles. I realized that I knew so many faces, yet no one deeply enough to weather the storm with me. That realization cut deep, leaving behind a pain that could not be ignored. But in the end, the pain of loneliness during trials became a teacher, an experience that reshaped me, forcing me to reevaluate the depth of my connections.

It challenged me to rise, not from the warmth of friendship, but from the burning heat of self-discovery. In a world where the silence of our phones can speak volumes, let our messages be a symphony of genuine care, empathy, and love. And let us never underestimate the power of the timeless question:

"How are you?"

To the one who has felt the ache of digital loneliness, who has scrolled through their contacts and feeds searching for connection only to be met with silence—you are not alone.

I know how it feels to send silent cries out for companionship, hoping someone will notice, someone will care enough to reach out. I know the sting of realizing that the friendships and connections you once trusted might not be as deep as you believed. The silence is heavy. It makes you question your worth, your place in the lives of others, your significance in a world that moves so quickly past your pain.

But hear me—YOUR VALUE IS NOT DETERMINED BY THE NUMBER OF MESSAGES YOU RECEIVE, THE NOTIFICATIONS THAT LIGHT UP YOUR SCREEN, OR THE RESPONSES (OR LACK THEREOF) TO YOUR VULNERABILITY. Your worth is not measured by how many people check in on you but by the undeniable truth that YOU MATTER, EVEN WHEN THE WORLD SEEMS TOO BUSY TO SAY IT.

I know the silence can be deafening, but do not let it deceive you into thinking you are forgotten. YAHWEH SEES YOU. He sees the loneliness that lingers in the spaces where friendship once thrived. He hears the unspoken prayers behind every unread message. And HE HAS NOT ABANDONED YOU.

This season of solitude may feel like a breaking, but what if it is actually a rebuilding? A refining? A calling to discover the friendships, the connections, the people who will truly stand with you, not just in moments of joy, but in the depths of struggle. THIS LONELINESS IS NOT THE END OF YOUR STORY—IT IS REVEALING THE KIND OF LOVE AND FRIENDSHIP WORTH HOLDING ONTO.

And if no one else has asked you today, let me be the one to say: HOW ARE YOU? Really. Because you deserve to be seen, heard, and valued. And even if the world feels distant, Yahweh is near. Keep holding on. YOU ARE NOT FORGOTTEN.

Discovering His Heart

Discovering His Heart

CHAPTER 12
UNRAVELING THE STORM WITHIN

During the storm that raged within me, I found temporary comfort in the safe house of my therapist's office. As I entered, the soft glow of muted lighting and the gentle hum of ambient sounds created a space where vulnerability was not only welcomed but encouraged. I sank into the comforting embrace of the plush armchair. My eyes met the steady gaze of Dr. Hagan, my guide, through the uncharted territories of my emotions.

The weight of my trauma loomed, a shadow that threatened to consume me, casting a darkness I struggled to navigate.

"I have been feeling things I cannot quite understand," I admitted, my voice a hesitant whisper in the quiet room.

Dr. Hagan, with a warmth that extended beyond words, nodded encouragingly.

"Feelings can be overwhelming," she said gently, "Especially when we encounter new and unexplored surfaces of our emotional landscape. It's okay to feel uncertain."

And in that moment of acknowledgment, the storm within me slowed, if only for a little while.

And so, the journey into the depths of my feelings began. Dr. Hagan, armed not with answers but with compassionate questions, guided me through the tangled web of emotions that had surfaced in the wake of my trauma. Each session unfolded like a carefully crafted map, charting the outlines of my internal terrain. Together, we navigated the waves of grief, resentment, and anxiety that crashed against the shores of my consciousness.

Discovering His Heart

During this process, Dr. Hagan was a steady anchor, allowing me to reach into the murky waters of emotions I had never acknowledged. It was both a painful unraveling and an emotional release, as I confronted the echoes of trauma that still resonated within me.

The therapeutic process was not a quick fix, nor was it a linear journey. Dr. Hagan, with unwavering patience, helped me peel back the layers of my emotional shield. She encouraged me to embrace the discomfort, recognizing that the very act of feeling was evidence of my resilience.

In the safe space of her office, I learned that acknowledging the intensity of my emotions was not a sign of weakness, but rather, a courageous act of self-compassion. Dr. Hagan introduced me to coping mechanisms, from mindfulness exercises to journaling, providing tools that became lamps guiding me through my emotional web.

As the weeks unfolded, the once-chaotic sea of emotions began to find a rhythm. Dr. Hagan's office became an asylum, a place where I could explore the depths of my feelings without judgment. She steered me toward a deeper understanding of myself and the trauma that had reshaped my emotional landscape. It was not about erasing my pain or magically transforming my emotions into something pleasant. Instead, the therapeutic journey became a process of integration, a coming to terms with the complexity of my feelings and learning to coexist with them. I soon discovered the strength to confront my shadows, knowing that in the acknowledgment of my emotions, I held the key to my own healing.

Discovering His Heart

With each therapeutic session, Dr. Hagan—my committed companion on this journey—continued to illuminate the path toward understanding and acceptance. Her office, once a realm of shadows, became a sacred space where the colors of my emotions could be explored, blended, and altered.

As we ventured deeper into the difficulties of my feelings, Dr. Hagan gently guided me to unearth the roots of my emotional responses. We navigated through memories and experiences, acknowledging the pain that had been concealed beneath layers of resistance. Her exploring questions were not invasive, they were invitations to unravel the knots within, fostering a sense of self-discovery. Together, we confronted fear, resentment, and sorrow that had taken residence in the chambers of my heart.

As I delved into my past, Dr. Hagan skillfully steered me toward self-compassion, a process of extending kindness to myself. She helped me to recognize that my emotional responses were not signs of weakness, but natural reactions to the trauma I had endured. She helped me to navigate the seas of self-forgiveness and acceptance. And I soon discovered that vulnerability was not a flaw, but a gateway to resilience.

Through thoughtful exercises and open dialogues, she skillfully guided me in creating a story that acknowledged the pain of my past while empowering me to rewrite the script for my future. It was not about erasing history, but reframing it, allowing my scars to become stories of survival and triumph. The art of healing began to take shape, reflecting the shades of my strength, resilience, and newfound understanding.

And so, with each visit to the office, I continued to stitch together the art of healing—a testament to the transformative power of confronting, exploring, and embracing the depths of my emotions. The colors of my emotional landscape, once muted by pain, now vibrantly painted the canvas of my evolving story, creating a story of strength, growth, and self-love. The office, once a confessional of pain, transformed into a shell, a refuge from the storm within, became a space where I learned to navigate the emotional storm and, ultimately, to emerge with a newfound understanding of my own strength in a cocoon of transformation.

In the gradual unfolding of my therapeutic journey, I began to see the emergence of a flexible caterpillar, one who had navigated the maze of emotions and surfaced with newfound resilience. The therapist's office, once an asylum for vulnerabilities, had become a forge, where the raw materials of pain were shaped into instruments of healing.

Our conversations surpassed the surface, diving into the core of my being, where my spirit lived and struggled to be free. Together, we explored not just the wounds, but the inherent strength that had carried me through the storms. We revisited the traumatic experiences, not to dwell in the pain, but to acknowledge the seeds of strength that had sprouted in the depths of adversity.

I confronted the shadows of the past with a newfound clarity. I dismantled self-limiting beliefs and reconstructed my story, one that did not mourn brokenness but celebrated resilience. I cultivated an arsenal of coping mechanisms, each tool a brushstroke on the canvas of my healing. The colors of my emotional palette, once restless and confused, now blended harmoniously. No longer a chaotic swirl of pain, but a portrait of emotional well-being. And under her guidance, I learned to craft my own masterpiece, a story not of suffering, but of self-empowerment, growth, and the quiet triumph of healing.

My healing journey was not without obstacles. There were moments of vulnerability, echoes of past pain that resonated unexpectedly. Yet, armed with the tools received in therapy, I confronted these echoes with a resistance that surprised even me. I was equipped not only with understanding but with practical strategies to navigate the inevitable fluctuations of healing.

As I stepped outside the therapist's office after each session, I carried with me a renewed sense of self. The emotions, once turbulent and overwhelming, now flowed with a graceful rhythm. I noticed subtle shifts in my responses to life's challenges, a testament to the internal transformation that had taken root within me.

My process with Dr. Hagan was not about erasing the scars, but about infusing them with significance. She helped me see the scars not as wounds to hide, but as marks of endurance and resilience. The echoes of trauma, once haunting, now harmonized with the symphony of my inner strength. Dr. Hagan, with profound insight and unwavering support, had been an instrumental conductor in this symphony of healing, a guide who had helped me rediscover the melody within.

To the one who has walked through the doors of a therapist's office, carrying the weight of unspoken pain, unsure

if healing was even possible—YOU ARE NOT ALONE.

I know what it feels like to sit in that chair, hesitant, afraid to unravel what has been buried for so long. I know the courage it takes to say, "I DON'T UNDERSTAND WHAT I'M FEELING," and to trust someone enough to guide you through the storm within. And I want you to know this: THE FACT THAT YOU ARE HERE, SEEKING HEALING, IS ALREADY PROOF OF YOUR STRENGTH.

Your pain is real, but so is your resilience. The emotions that once felt chaotic and overwhelming are not your enemies—they are messengers, revealing truths about your heart, your past, and your capacity to heal. Every session, every conversation, every moment of vulnerability is not a sign of weakness, but of transformation.

Healing is not about erasing the past, but about reclaiming your story. YOU ARE NOT DEFINED BY WHAT HAPPENED TO YOU. You are defined by the way you rise, by the way you choose to face your pain with courage instead of silence. Your scars do not diminish you, they tell the story of your survival, of the battles you have fought, of the strength that has carried you forward even when you thought you couldn't take another step.

So keep going. Keep showing up for yourself. Keep trusting that this journey—though painful, though uncertain—is leading you toward something greater than you ever imagined. ONE DAY, YOU WILL LOOK BACK AND SEE THAT THE STORM DID NOT DESTROY YOU. IT SHAPED YOU. And you, my friend, are becoming something powerful, something whole, something deeply, beautifully healed.

YOU ARE NOT ALONE IN THIS. YOU ARE STRONGER THAN YOU KNOW. KEEP GOING.

Discovering His Heart

Discovering His Heart

CHAPTER 13
FORGED IN FIRE: TURNING PAIN INTO POWER

In the chaotic consequences of my divorce, I stood at the edge of an unfamiliar and disorienting expanse, a sea of uncertainty stretching infinitely before me. The once reliable compass of my life lay shattered, its pieces scattered like shards of glass, leaving me directionless in the vast unknown. The map I had meticulously crafted for my future was now a tattered relic, its once-clear pathways obscured by the ragged edges of broken dreams and unfulfilled promises.

The pain that consumed me transcended the physical realm, reaching into the depths of my emotional and spiritual core. It was a relentless storm, a storm of suffering that threatened to engulf me in its all-encompassing darkness. Each wave of heartbreak and disappointment crashed over me, leaving me gasping for breath in the turbulent sea of my own emotions.

The dissolution of my marriage felt like losing a part of myself. It was not just the end of a legal agreement, but the shattering of dreams, the dismantling of shared memories, and the destruction of a once-secure foundation. I felt lost, like a ship without a captain, drifting in a vast ocean of solitude. The familiar rhythm of my daily life became an incompatible symphony, and the future seemed like a deep void.

Yet, in this overwhelming abyss, I stumbled upon an unexpected lifeline, one that would become my anchor: CrossFit and weightlifting.

After a week of grueling workouts, I learned that CrossFit was more than just exercise. It was a fitness regimen known for its intensity and community spirit. It was a leap into the unknown, a desperate attempt to rescue a fragment of control over my life. What began as a physical outlet for pain would soon become a place where I could channel my pain into purpose, and my vulnerability into strength, and also a pathway to resilience, transformation, and rediscovery.

Weightlifting, an integral part of CrossFit, became my stabilizing force amidst the turbulent sea. The cold steel of the barbell became my instrument for the chaotic emotions raging within me. Each lift was not just physical exertion, it was a symbolic raising of the burdens that weighed down my soul. The barbell, with its unforgiving weight, demanded my focus, forcing me to be present in the moment. In the act of lifting, I found a temporary escape from the haunting shadows of my past.

CrossFit, with its constantly varied, high-intensity workouts, presented me with a challenge that surpassed the physical. As I pushed my body to its limits, I discovered a reservoir of strength within myself that I never knew existed. The pain of each burpee, the burn of every assault bike sprint, and the struggle of each pull-up mirrored the emotional anguish I was experiencing. Yet, with each completed workout, I emerged stronger—physically and mentally.

One of the unexpected gifts of CrossFit was the sense of community that surrounded me. In a room filled with sweat and determination, I found a tribe, a family of like-minded individuals, each facing their own battles. The friendship extended beyond the gym walls, it became my support network, my lifeline that pulled me from the depths of my depression. Our struggles forged bonds, stronger than any weight lifted.

And the encouragement of my new community became the comfort my suffering spirit desperately needed.

In the chaos of divorce, where every aspect of my life seemed uncertain, CrossFit gave me structure. The daily workouts became a routine, a series of challenges I could expect and conquer. The discipline of showing up at the box mirrored the discipline I needed to rebuild my fractured life. As the days turned into weeks, and the weeks into months, I found comfort in the rhythmic cadence of my training.

Weightlifting became a representation of my emotional journey. The first time I lifted a weight that once seemed impossible, it was not just a physical triumph, it was a symbolic victory over the weight of my past. The barbell became a tool of empowerment, an instrument through which I channeled my pain into power. Each clean, each jerk, each snatch, was a statement that I was not defined by my damage but by my ability to rise from the ashes.

I found a new sense of purpose. The pursuit of physical excellence became a metaphor for the pursuit of personal growth. Setting goals in the gym translated to setting goals in my personal and professional life. The discipline needed to master complex movements mirrored the discipline needed to rebuild my shattered identity. The mental fortitude needed to push through a grueling workout was mirrored in the resilience needed to navigate the complexities of my divorce.

In the sweat-soaked silence of the gym, I found clarity. As I broke through physical plateaus, I simultaneously shattered the mental barriers that had confined me. The victories in the gym became evidence of the unbreakable spirit within, proving that I was not a victim of circumstances but a survivor with the power to redefine my story. In the relentless pursuit of improvement, I unearthed a roadmap to redemption.

CrossFit and weightlifting did not erase the pain of my divorce, but they provided me with the tools to navigate it. The barbell became my therapist. The box became my asylum, a sacred space where I shed the earlier version of myself and rose as a phoenix from the flames that had been consuming me.

In the clanging of weight plates and the rhythmic thump of jump ropes, I found a soundtrack for my recovery. The weights I lifted were not just physical, they were the burdens of my past, lifted with each act of defiance against depression. I rediscovered my strength, my resilience, and the ability to rebuild.

As the days turned into months, my dedication to training evolved from a coping mechanism into a passionate pursuit. The gym, once a reserve for self-finding, transformed into an arena where I pursued not just redemption but excellence. The muscle memory of routine that initially gave me support became the foundation for a competitive spirit I never knew existed within me.

I shifted from a casual participant to a competitive athlete, a delicate yet sincere transformation. It began with the realization that my journey was not just about personal healing, it was an opportunity to push boundaries and redefine my own limitations. The familiar faces at the box, once companions in the battle against personal demons, became friendly competitors

Discovering His Heart

in the pursuit of athletic mastery.

The CrossFit Open, an annual competition uniting athletes worldwide, became my gateway to competitive admiration. What started as a personal challenge to measure progress soon transformed into a quest for domination. The thrill of competing against thousands—each striving for their personal best—fueled a fire within me. Under the shimmering glow of the gym's fluorescent lights, I discovered a stage where the transformation unfolding within me could finally be displayed.

The Open workouts, shrouded in mystery, proved to be more than just physical tests; they were mental trials as well. The community that once provided comfort now served as my cheering squad, urging me to shatter my own expectations. Every thruster, every box jump, every pull-up—and even the dreaded assault bike—became a testament to the resilience I had cultivated over time. The Open was not merely competition against others; it was a battle against the haunting doubts that whispered in the corners of my mind.

As my performance in the Open soared, so did my ambitions. The CrossFit Open Quarterfinals—an arena that separated the elite from the resolute—became my next stage. The workouts grew more demanding, and the competition, fiercer. It was no longer solely about personal redemption; it had evolved into a pursuit of excellence, a chance to stand shoulder to shoulder with the best and realize the athlete I aspired to become.

Simultaneously, my journey in weightlifting took a competitive turn. What had begun as therapeutic lifts, each rep a means of channeling pain, soon transformed into calculated attempts to break personal records and earn national recognition. The sound of the barbell hitting the platform no longer echoed just within the walls of my gym; it resonated through the weightlifting community, a declaration of my relentless pursuit of excellence.

Competing at local events became my steppingstone to the national stage, where the stakes were higher and the demands more relentless. The path to elite competition required more than just strength—it demanded sacrifices. The suffering of precise, unforgiving training, the discipline of meticulously planned nutrition, and the mental fortitude to push beyond physical and emotional barriers became the price of admission to the competitive arena. Yet, with every sacrifice came an undeniable sense of purpose. The thrill of a successful lift, the roar of the crowd, and the acknowledgment of my peers became rewards that transcended the pain of the journey.

The culmination of my efforts came in the form of a national ranking in weightlifting. The once-aimless wanderer had found his place among the nation's elite lifters—an achievement that was more than just numbers on a scoreboard. It was a testament to the transformative power of resilience, proof that pain could be repurposed into strength. The medals and honors, while tangible symbols of success, were merely reflections of the true victories—the battles I had fought and won within myself.

Competing at the highest levels of CrossFit and weightlifting taught me invaluable lessons that transcended the sport itself.

Every missed lift, every failed attempt, and each moment of self-doubt was not a setback but an opportunity for growth. The competitive arena became more than just a test of physical ability—it became a mirror reflecting the depths of my character.

As an athlete, I embraced a mentality that extended far beyond the gym or the competition floor. The discipline, resilience, and unyielding focus I cultivated through training became guiding principles in every area of my life. The skills I sharpened—time management, goal setting, mental toughness—proved to be just as vital in the boardroom, in relationships, and in every aspect of my redefined existence.

What started as a refuge in CrossFit and weightlifting transformed into a catalyst for my personal rebirth. From the ashes of a broken marriage, I did not just survive—I evolved. I became a competitor, an athlete who found solace, purpose, and redemption within the four walls of the gym. The medals, the national rank, and the applause were never the ultimate destination. The real victory was in the transformation itself, the realization that the pain of divorce, the sense of loss, and the shattered identity no longer defined me.

I am not the same person who first stepped into that box on that fateful day. I am stronger—not just in body, but in spirit.

The scars of divorce remain, but they no longer define me. Through the relentless pursuit of strength, I found healing. CrossFit and weightlifting were not just exercises; they became the transformation that turned pain into power, despair into determination, and loss into a triumphant new beginning. The competitive arena became a canvas where I painted the portrait of my resilience, each stroke a testament to the journey from despair to triumph.

But through this journey, I also came to understand that competition was never the destination, it was the vehicle. Beyond the weights, beyond the sweat, beyond the applause, I discovered the essence of my own strength. The gym, once a sanctuary for healing, became a temple of resilience, a testament to the invincible spirit that lives within each of us, waiting to be awakened by the clang of the plates and the roar of the crowd.

In the end, it was not about lifting heavier or ranking higher. It was about lifting myself out of the darkness, proving to myself that I am more than my past, stronger than my struggles, and capable of building a future that is not defined by loss but by limitless possibility.

To the one who has stood at the edge of devastation, feeling the weight of loss and the uncertainty of what comes next— YOU ARE NOT ALONE.

I know what it's like to feel directionless, as if the life you once knew has crumbled, leaving you staring at the wreckage, unsure of how to rebuild. I know the ache of shattered dreams and the loneliness that follows when everything familiar feels foreign. BUT I ALSO KNOW THIS—YOUR STORY IS NOT OVER.

What started as pain has the power to become fuel. EVERY WEIGHT YOU LIFT, EVERY MOVEMENT FORWARD, EVERY OUNCE OF STRENGTH YOU DISCOVER IN

YOURSELF IS PROOF THAT YOU ARE NOT BROKEN—YOU ARE BECOMING. You are refining yourself in the fire of hardship, forging a resilience that will carry you through more than just the gym, but through life itself.

Your healing will not be linear. Some days will be filled with victories, and others will remind you of the scars that remain. But with each rep, each challenge, and each goal met, you are proving that YOU ARE STRONGER THAN WHAT TRIED TO BREAK YOU. The gym, the weights, the discipline—it's not just about competition. It's about proving to yourself that YOUR IDENTITY is not defined by what you lost but by what you are building.

Keep going. Keep pushing. Keep discovering the strength that has always been inside of you. YOU ARE NOT A VICTIM OF YOUR PAST—YOU ARE A WARRIOR RISING FROM IT. And one day, you'll look back and realize that the pain that once tried to bury you became the very force that made you unstoppable.

YOU ARE NOT JUST SURVIVING. YOU ARE CONQUERING

Discovering His Heart

Discovering His Heart

CHAPTER 14
A LIFE IN MOTION, A SOUL AT REST

This solitude was not an emptiness but a deep reservoir—a space where I found the echoes of my thoughts and the quiet rhythms of self-discovery. It was a paradox, a coexistence of both loneliness and fulfillment. On the surface, my life was structured, predictable, and filled with movement—yet beneath it, there existed an undercurrent of something unspoken, an invisible dialogue between who I was and who I was becoming.

The passing of two years marked not just the passage of time but an evolution of self. The loneliness that once seemed like a shadow lurking on the edges of my reality had, in some ways, become a part of me—a familiar presence rather than an unwelcome guest. It no longer signified a lack but a sharpening, a refining fire that burned away distraction and left me face-to-face with my own essence.

Through work, workouts, and coaching CrossFit, I learned that solitude was not an exile—it was a teacher. In the absence of constant external validation, I was forced to seek inward. In the discipline of my daily grind, I found a structure that kept me moving forward. And in the quiet moments between tasks, I found my sanctuary, a space where the world grew still enough for me to listen, not to the noise of my past, but to the whisper of my future.

This solitude was not an empty void but a structured existence—a life meticulously built upon the foundation of discipline and movement. The alarm clock's melody, the cadence of work, the rhythm of my workouts, and the cycle of coaching all intertwined into a predictable symphony. Each note played with precision; each movement rehearsed to the point of muscle memory. Yet, within the structured repetition, there existed a profound stillness—an awareness of my own presence within the routine.

I found myself thriving in this solitude, though not untouched by its weight. It was a delicate balance between productivity and introspection, a place where silence could be both a refuge and a reminder. The loneliness that once felt oppressive had transformed into an unspoken ally—a companion that allowed me to sit with my own thoughts without the desperate need for distraction. I became attuned to the spaces between the noise, the quiet moments that carried the echoes of past experiences and the whispers of untapped potential.

Coaching others offered glimpses of connection, a temporary escape from the inward journey. I poured into my athletes, pushing them beyond their perceived limits, celebrating their victories as if they were my own. Yet, even in the shared energy of the gym, I remained an observer in my own life—engaged, yet standing just outside the circle, watching rather than fully immersing.

The structure of my days ensured progress. The repetition fostered discipline. But in the margins of that carefully crafted existence, a question lingered—was I merely surviving within the rhythm of routine, or was I building toward something greater? Was this solitude a season of growth, or had it become a comfortable prison of my own making?

The weight of that question did not demand an immediate answer, but it settled within me, waiting for the moment I would be ready to face it. Until then, I continued moving—lifting, coaching, working—navigating the paradox of solitude and purpose, discipline and longing, structure and the quiet unknown.

And yet, as much as this structured solitude gave me stability, it also carried an unspoken weight. The absence of loneliness did not necessarily equate to fulfillment. It became a paradox, a life so well-orchestrated that it left little room for surprise, for deviation, for the very things that often give life their richness. I had mastered the art of moving forward without truly feeling the steps beneath me.

I found myself questioning whether this life of precision and control was a shield or a cage. Was I protecting myself from the unpredictability of human connection, or was I unintentionally numbing myself to the possibilities beyond routine? The very discipline that had once saved me from the wreckage of my past now stood as both my greatest asset and my quietest adversary.

Even in the midst of my solitude, I recognized that true growth does not come from mere survival—it comes from stepping beyond the predictable. It comes from allowing vulnerability to seep into the cracks of even the most well-constructed walls. It comes from moments that disrupt routine, from relationships that challenge the carefully built barriers, from experiences that force reflection beyond the structured confines of repetition.

Perhaps the question was not whether my solitude was sustainable, but whether I was willing to let the automatic mode shift—just enough to invite the unexpected. To let the rigid lines of my life blur ever so slightly. To allow for the kind of human connection that could exist beyond the carefully controlled parameters I had set.

Because maybe, just maybe, solitude was never meant to be a permanent state, but rather a season—one that had given me strength, but also one that, in time, I would need to leave behind.

In that moment of deviation—standing amidst the stillness of a snow-covered mountain, surrounded by friends yet oddly distant, I felt the weight of my solitude in a way I had not before. The contrast between the warmth of companionship and the comfort of my routine became glaringly evident. For the first time in a long time, I was aware of the walls I had built around myself, not in resistance to others, but as a means of survival.

The weekend at Big Bear became more than just a trip; it was a mirror. It reflected back at me the unspoken truth I had buried beneath the discipline of my daily life. My carefully structured world had served its purpose, it had given me strength, clarity, and direction, but in its unwavering consistency, it had also numbed me to the richness of spontaneous connection. The realization was both unsettling and liberating.

As I stepped outside that morning, watching the storm settle over the landscape, I understood that true resilience was not found in isolation, nor in routine alone, but in the willingness to engage with the world beyond my own design. It was in the ability to welcome the unpredictability of relationships, to step beyond the controlled environment I had meticulously crafted,

Discovering His Heart

and to allow life to unfold in its natural rhythm.

I would always carry the discipline, the focus, and the solitude that had once been my refuge. But I also knew that balance was essential—that true growth required both structure and spontaneity, both solitude and connection. The automatic mode that had sustained me for so long had to evolve, not into chaos, but into something more alive, more open, more human.

As I left Big Bear and returned to the familiarity of my life, I did so with a new awareness—that the journey was not just about endurance, but about embracing the fullness of experience. And perhaps, in learning to let go, I would discover something even greater than what I had built on my own.

To the one who has found strength in solitude, yet wonders if it has become a cage—YOU ARE NOT ALONE.

There is beauty in discipline, in routine, in the structured life that has carried you through the wreckage of the past. You have learned to stand firm, to rely on yourself, to become someone who moves forward even when the weight of the world presses down. That is no small thing—it is a testament to your resilience, to your ability to take what was broken and build something steadily.

But hear me—YOU WERE NEVER MEANT TO STAY IN SURVIVAL MODE FOREVER.

Solitude has been your teacher, your safe place, but growth does not stop there. There is another kind of strength waiting for you—the kind that comes from stepping beyond the predictable, from letting life surprise you, from allowing the presence of others to soften the edges of your well-constructed world.

It is okay to open the door, even if just a little. To let the walls blur. To embrace moments of connection that do not demand control, but simply asks you to be present. You are not losing yourself by allowing others in—you are expanding, evolving, discovering that TRUE STRENGTH IS NOT JUST IN STANDING ALONE, BUT IN KNOWING WHEN TO LEAN INTO THE WARMTH OF SHARED EXPERIENCE.

So take your time. Move at your own pace. But know this—THERE IS A LIFE BEYOND THE LINES YOU HAVE DRAWN, AND IT IS WAITING FOR YOU. A life that is not just structured, but full. A LIFE WHERE SOLITUDE IS NOT EXILE, BUT A CHOICE AMONG MANY, WHERE CONNECTION DOES NOT THREATEN YOUR STRENGTH, BUT DEEPENS IT.

You have learned to survive. Now, allow yourself to LIVE.

Discovering His Heart

CHAPTER 15
BORROWED TIME, BORROWED SPACES

Each Airbnb stay became a brief chapter in my unfolding story—an address that shifted as often as the emotions within me. I was not simply moving from one place to another; I was running, escaping the silent echoes of what once was. Every space was a fleeting sanctuary, offering the illusion of stability while underscoring the reality of my transience.

The nights were the hardest. Lying in unfamiliar beds, staring at ceilings that held no memories, I wrestled with the weight of displacement. Home was no longer a physical place, it was a concept that had become abstract, something I could no longer define. The ache of missing my children, of not tucking them in at night or hearing their laughter fill the walls, settled in my chest like an unshakable burden.

Homelessness after divorce was not just about lacking a permanent address; it was about losing the sense of belonging that home once provided. I became a nomad, not just in the physical world but in my own identity. Who was I now, outside of the life I had built? Without the structure of family and familiarity, I was left to redefine myself, to piece together a version of me that could stand independently in the absence of everything I once held dear.

Yet, in the solitude of my wandering, I found unexpected lessons. Each new place forced me to adapt, to embrace uncertainty, to find stability within myself rather than in the walls that surrounded me. The discomfort of constant change became a teacher, revealing the resilience I never knew I had. I learned to live lightly, to let go of material attachments, and to find presence in the moment, rather than in the longing for what had been.

There were moments of deep loneliness, but also moments of profound self-discovery. In the absence of routine, I found space for reflection. In the lack of permanence, I found the strength to rebuild—not a home of bricks and mortar, but a foundation within myself that could weather any storm.

The journey of homelessness after divorce was not just about finding a new place to live, it was about finding a new way to exist. It was about transforming the pain of loss into the power of reinvention. And as I moved from one temporary home to another, I realized that home was never just a place—it was the people we love, the memories we carry, and, ultimately, the person we become in the face of life's most unexpected turns.

Home—once a sanctuary—became a battlefield of memories, both beautiful and painful. The familiar walls, once a source of comfort, now felt like a prison, tightening around me with every passing day. Stability, once cherished, became an unbearable weight. In the wake of divorce, my decision to leave wasn't just a logistical step; it was an act of emotional survival.

I abandoned the notion of a fixed address, turning instead to the transient solace of Airbnb rentals, booking accommodations one week at a time. Each new space offered a fleeting sense of refuge—comfortable, but never quite home. The thought of settling, of building a routine in an empty house absent the laughter of children, was too much to bear. So, I chose movement.

Discovering His Heart

The Airbnb circuit became my lifeline—a rotating series of temporary shelters shielding me from the storm within. Each fresh location carried the illusion of a new beginning, a brief escape from the relentless echoes of a life I once knew. Yet, the very impermanence of these spaces only reinforced the transience that had become my reality.

Living in Airbnbs meant living on borrowed time. Every stay came with a countdown, the ticking clock of both my reservation and my healing. I found strange comfort in the ritual—come Sunday, I would pack my bags and move on, leaving behind the weight of yesterday's shadows, if only for a little while longer.

As the weeks passed, the pain of being away from home—however transient—deepened. The silence of my rented spaces became unbearable, filled with the imagined echoes of my children's laughter. The emptiness pressed in, suffocating. Some nights, the weight of it all drove me to sleep in my car rather than on the bed inside my rental. For a time, my car became more than just transportation—it was my asylum on wheels, a cocoon of isolation where I could momentarily set the world aside.

I sought solace in the stillness of secluded parking spots, under the quiet glow of the moon. There was a strange peace in those moments, but even the open sky could not replace the warmth of the home I had lost. That absence lingered, heavy in the silence of the night.

In search of relief, I often found myself driving northward, toward Covelo. The journey was more than just a physical trip, it was a pilgrimage of sorts, a search for connection and comfort. Covelo, where my children lived with their mother, became both a refuge and a reminder of what was missing. The landscapes, vast and unspoiled, mirrored the ache in my heart, offering both beauty and solitude.

Each visit was dictated by my agreement with their mother, yet the real calendar was my longing. The anticipation of seeing their faces—so full of life, so essential to my healing—became my anchor. Each reunion was a collision of joy and grief, a momentary restoration of what once was, shadowed by the reality of our separation.

The road itself became a kind of therapist, stretching endlessly before me, offering space to process the storm inside. In the solitude of the drive, my thoughts wandered through the labyrinth of identity, purpose, and the elusive meaning of home. Each mile wasn't just distance traveled, it was a step deeper into self-discovery, a silent reckoning with my new reality.

Along the way, nature became my silent confidant. The rustling leaves, the murmuring rivers, the towering trees, they bore quiet witness to my struggles. In their presence, I found brief moments of peace, a reminder that even in brokenness, there is still beauty. And perhaps, in time, healing too.

The journey through homelessness after my divorce—marked by temporary housing, sleepless nights in my car, and long drives northward—became a test of my spirit's endurance. In the absence of a physical home, I was forced to search for one within myself. The path to healing and self-discovery unfolded amidst ever-changing landscapes and fleeting accommodations, each stop along the way shaping me in ways I never expected.

As weeks turned into months, the scars of my past began to fade, giving way to a new sense of self—one forged through adversity, yet strengthened by it. This journey became a testament to the resilience I found in vulnerability, to the quiet strength hidden in my deepest despair. It revealed not just my ability to survive, but my capacity to rebuild, even when the very notion of home felt fractured beyond repair.

More than anything, it was a story of transformation—of survival, growth, and an unwavering hope that, despite life's uncertainty, my true home could always be found within His heart, the only place vast enough to carry the weight of my journey.

To the one who has walked through the storm of displacement, whose journey has been marked by borrowed spaces and sleepless nights, you are not alone.

You have endured the ache of transience, of searching for home in places that were never meant to hold you. You have packed and unpacked not just your bags, but the weight of your emotions, carrying them from one place to another, hoping that somewhere along the way, you might find rest.

And yet, through the instability, through the solitude, through the unbearable quiet of unfamiliar walls—you have survived. You have learned that home is not just a structure of wood and stone, but a resilience that lives within you. HOME IS NOT LOST, IT IS BEING REBUILT—ONE STEP, ONE

BREATH, ONE MOMENT OF SELF-DISCOVERY AT A TIME.

Your journey has not been easy, but it has been shaping you. The miles you have traveled, the spaces you have rested in, the moments of longing that felt like they might break you—THEY HAVE NOT BEEN IN VAIN. They are proof of your endurance, your ability to keep moving forward even when the road ahead feels uncertain.

And though the past may echo in the empty spaces, though the ache of what was may still linger, YOU ARE NOT FORGOTTEN, AND YOU ARE NOT FORSAKEN. Yahweh has been with you in every temporary home, in every quiet night, in every drive northward. His presence has been the shelter you could not see, the steady hand guiding you through this wilderness.

So hold on. KEEP WALKING, KEEP SEARCHING, KEEP BELIEVING. You are not defined by what you have lost, but by the strength you are finding in the process. And in time, when you look back, you will see that this season—though painful—was never about the loss of home, but about discovering the foundation of who you truly are.

You are not homeless. YOU ARE ON YOUR WAY HOME.

Discovering His Heart

CHAPTER 16
BATTLES FOUGHT IN THE DARK

Discovering His Heart

    The night stretched endlessly before me; a vast canvas of darkness painted with memories that refused to fade. Sleep, an elusive companion, hovered just beyond my reach, teasing me with the promise of rest yet never surrendering to my grasp. I was ensnared in the clutches of sleepless nights, where the echoes of my trauma carved deeper into the fabric of my consciousness. While the world around me surrendered to slumber, I remained entangled in the maze of my own thoughts, wandering through corridors lined with whispers of the past.

    The silence of the night magnified everything—the unspoken words, the buried emotions, the weight of sorrow pressing down like an unbearable shroud. Each breath felt shallow; each sighed a quiet plea for relief that never came. Shadows stretched long in the moonlit glow filtering through my window, illuminating the specters that lurked in the recesses of my mind.

    My trauma, relentless and unyielding, cast its shadow over my every attempt to find solace in the embrace of sleep. My bed, once a refuge, had become a battlefield where the war against memory played out in endless cycles. The steady tick of the clock echoed like the drumbeat of my restless mind—each second stretching into eternity, each moment a reminder that dawn was still painfully distant.

    And so, the hours marched forward, relentless and unfeeling, dragging me through the hollow corridors of another sleepless night.

    In the stillness of each night, I wrestled with the flashes of my past. Faces and scenes flickered through my mind like a distorted Instagram reel—each frame, a vivid reminder of the trauma woven into the fabric of my story. Sleep, an elusive prey, slipped through my desperate fingers, retreating further with every restless hour. The bedroom walls, silent witnesses to my inner turmoil, seemed to close in, as if bearing the weight of my unspoken struggle.

Darkness, once a peaceful backdrop to my dreams, had become a breeding ground for shadows—specters that lurked in the periphery of my consciousness, waiting to be acknowledged. These nights were a reckoning, a forced confrontation with the aftermath of pain that refused to be ignored. And as dawn's first light crept through the curtains, I found myself standing at the edge of another day, staring into the abyss of what lay ahead.

Each sleepless night was a journey through the tangled web of my own suffering, a relentless testament to the resilience required to navigate the depths of my inner darkness. The same trauma that robbed me of rest also revealed a hidden strength—a quiet force that had long been buried beneath the wreckage of my past, waiting to be recognized.

With each sunrise came a hesitant relief, as though the night had finally loosened its grip on my weary soul. The remnants of sleepless hours clung to the edges of my mind, yet the daylight offered a fragile truce—a chance to gather the scattered pieces of my restless thoughts. Mornings carried a silence unlike the night's, a calm after the storm, an exhale after the fight.

It was in this stillness that I began sifting through the emotional wreckage. Like a hurricane, my trauma had carved deep scars into the silhouette of my soul, and in the softened glow of morning, I could feel their weight. Yet, as I sat with the echoes of the night, a quiet realization emerged, these sleepless hours were not merely a descent into suffering. They were an act of defiance. A bold, unspoken confrontation with my past. Each moment spent wrestling with the shadows was a step toward healing, a testament to the resilience that had always been within me, waiting to rise.

Each morning became a canvas for self-compassion, a quiet reminder that healing is not always linear. Every sleepless night was not a defeat, but a battle fought, a testament to the truth that the scars of trauma do not fade easily. In the hush of dawn, I learned to embrace the fragility of my own kindness—to understand that recovery is a journey marked by restless nights and incremental victories. Each day stretched before me like an open road, inviting me to carry the lessons of the night into the unfolding hours. It was a call to acknowledge the strength found in vulnerability and to seek support in the sacred work of healing.

The shadows that once loomed ominously over my sleepless nights now softened in the morning light, no longer threats but quiet reminders—proof that even in my darkest moments, the seeds of growth and renewal had been planted.

As each day unfolded, it wove a tapestry of both struggle and resilience. The remnants of sleepless nights lingered in the background; subtle echoes of the emotional journey undertaken in the solitude before dawn. Moving through the routines of daily life felt like a delicate dance—each step a conscious effort to honor the vulnerability exposed in the depths of the night. The rhythm of my world, its familiar chaos, seemed to mirror the steady cadence of my heartbeat—each thrum carrying whispers of the hours spent awake, wrestling with the past.

And yet, something had shifted. My trauma, once a looming shadow lurking in the recesses of my mind, had become something else entirely—a subject of reflection rather than fear. I began to see that every sleepless night had served as a vessel, forging a deeper understanding of the wounds that demanded attention and the quiet strength that emerged from acknowledging their existence.

The vulnerability of the night had given birth to something unexpected: compassion. A compassion that reached beyond my own struggles, allowing me to recognize the silent battles waged by others. In my own suffering, I had found the capacity to see, to understand, and to extend grace—not just to myself, but to the weary souls who, like me, walked the delicate path between darkness and light.

As the sun dipped below the horizon, painting the sky in hues of warmth, I found comfort in a quiet realization—each sleepless night had not been a solitary journey. Instead, it had tethered me to the shared human experience, where restless nights were not anomalies but familiar chapters in the story of resilience. In the hush of each evening, I allowed myself a moment to breathe, to acknowledge the progress made. The trauma that once cast an unrelenting shadow over my nights met with quiet courage. Each sleepless hour, rather than a thief of peace, had become a catalyst for a renewed sense of self. My scars remained, not erased, but transformed—worn as badges of perseverance, testaments to the endurance found in the heart of vulnerability.

With every approaching nightfall, I embraced the prospect of rest with a newfound humility. Each sleepless night had taught me that healing is not a straight path but a mosaic of moments—both broken and whole—shaping the silhouette of strength. The trauma, though once an unrelenting adversary, had unwillingly become a force that refined my resilience.

And through it all, I held onto His truth—the quiet revelation imprinted in the courage it took to face the shadows and still rise, however weary, into the dawn of a new day.

In the embrace of the night, I found something unexpected: gratitude. Gratitude for the strength discovered in the struggle, for the lessons carved into the fabric of my journey, and for His promise—that beyond the weight of darkness, a new day always awaited. This was more than just a chapter in my story; it was a testament to the courage found in confronting the night, a quiet acknowledgment that even in the darkest hours, healing lingers in the wings of the approaching light.

To the one who lies awake in the stillness of the night, wrestling with thoughts that refuse to let go—You are not alone.

The weight of your past may press heavily against your chest, and the echoes of your trauma may weave through the silence, making the night feel endless. But hear this: **THE DARKNESS DOES NOT DEFINE YOU.** These sleepless nights, though painful, are not proof of your defeat—they are proof of your endurance. Each one is a quiet testament to the strength you possess, to the resilience that refuses to be extinguished.

You may feel like a prisoner to these restless hours, but even here, in the solitude of the night, something sacred is unfolding. YOUR SURVIVAL IS NOT PASSIVE—IT IS A COURAGEOUS ACT. With every moment you spend confronting the shadows of your past, you are not drowning; you are fighting. And that fight, no matter how exhausting, is leading you toward healing.

Know this: YOUR PAIN IS NOT WASTED. The nights that stretch too long, the weight you carry in the quiet, the longing for peace that feels just out of reach—it is all shaping you, refining you, making way for a dawn that will come. And when that dawn arrives, when

the first light spills across your weary soul, you will see what the night has been building within you. A STRENGTH YOU NEVER KNEW YOU HAD. A RESILIENCE THAT WILL CARRY YOU FORWARD.

And above all, YOU ARE NOT FORGOTTEN. Yahweh sees you in these long nights, in the restless turning, in the quiet tears. He holds you even when you feel most alone, whispers peace even when the silence is deafening. He has not left you in this darkness—He is walking through it with you, leading you toward the light.

So hold on, dear soul. KEEP BREATHING. KEEP ENDURING. KEEP RISING. The night will not last forever, and when the morning comes, you will not just be standing— you will be stronger than ever before.

Discovering His Heart

CHAPTER 17
NOT ANSWERS, BUT UNDERSTANDING

Discovering His Heart

Sunday after Sunday, I sought solace within the hallowed halls of the church. With each echoing hymn and every verse recited, I searched for answers to the struggles that shadowed my days. Bible study sessions became more than opportunities for learning—they became a lifeline, a desperate pursuit of understanding. I combed through sacred verses, hoping to find the key that would unlock the mysteries of my life. I yearned for guidance, for a divine roadmap to navigate the chaotic terrain of my challenges.

The prayers I whispered carried the weight of my desperation, pleas for revelation that might lift the burdens embedded deep within my heart. As I immersed myself in the services, the teachings, and the rhythm of worship, I felt fleeting moments of peace. The church became a sanctuary—a place where, if only for a short while, I could set aside the heaviness of my worries. In those shared moments of faith, I glimpsed a flicker of light, a promise that perhaps the answers I sought were hidden within the sacred texts and communal devotion.

Yet, with each passing week, I found myself entangled in contradictions. The more I pursued comfort in the church's embrace, the more elusive the answers became. The teachings, though profound, often felt distant—like ancient wisdom veiled in a language I struggled to decipher. I longed for clarity, for a direct response to the questions that echoed ceaselessly in my mind.

Bible study, once a source of hope, became an arena of internal conflict. The deeper I delved into scripture, the more I questioned whether the answers I sought were truly meant to be found within those pages. A subtle frustration crept into my soul, replacing the familiarity of comfort with a quiet sense of isolation. The church pews, once a place of refuge, began to feel like a place of longing—an unfulfilled desire for understanding that remained just beyond my reach.

One day, as I sat in the quiet solitude of the church after a service, a realization washed over me like a gentle tide: the answers I sought might not be neatly inscribed in ancient texts or echoed in collective prayers. Perhaps they existed as whispers of intuition, seeds of self-discovery waiting to take root within the depths of my own being. In that moment of revelation, I understood that my spiritual journey was not a straight path but a wandering exploration—one that required me to embrace uncertainty, to seek guidance not only from external sources but from the quiet wisdom within.

The church, once my refuge, became something else—a steppingstone. A sacred space where I learned that sometimes the answers I long for are not found in the destination but in the journey itself.

As I continued attending services, my relationship with faith underwent a profound shift. Sunday mornings became less about chasing immediate clarity and more about leaning into the process of self-discovery. The holy verses, once distant and enigmatic, began to resonate with a newfound authenticity. Bible study transformed from a quest for definitive solutions into a space for reflection, a chance to explore meaning rather than simply extract it. The discussions evolved into exchanges of personal experiences—testaments to the uniqueness of each person's struggles and the many ways in which faith weaves itself into our lives.

In the quiet moments between prayers and hymns, a subtle wisdom began to take shape within me. The answers I sought were not neatly packaged in doctrine but unfolded slowly, like the petals of a blooming rose. I came to realize that the church—with its rituals, teachings, and traditions—was not my destination, but my compass, guiding me through the uncharted wilderness of my soul.

As I let go of the expectation that revelation would strike like lightning, I began to listen for the whispers—the gentle nudges of insight that emerged in stillness. And in doing so, the perceived distance between my spiritual longing and the realities of my life began to narrow. The struggles that once felt like barriers transformed into steppingstones, leading me deeper into the depths of my own understanding.

I came to appreciate the beauty of diverse perspectives, recognizing that faith is not a singular path, but a tapestry woven from individual journeys. In my own internal wrestling, I discovered the quiet power of vulnerability. I began to share not just my triumphs but the raw, unfiltered struggles that shaped my spiritual walk. And as I did, something shifted. The church, which had once felt distant, slowly became a refuge—a space where authenticity was embraced, where the courage to be vulnerable became a source of strength rather than weakness.

The turning point did not arrive in the form of a grand revelation, but in a quiet moment of acceptance. I realized that the answers I pursued were not external validations, but internal awakenings. Faith was not a shield against struggles, but a lantern illuminating the path through them.

As I continued to attend church and engage in Bible study, a quiet peace settled within me. My struggles did not vanish, but their weight changed. They became catalysts for growth, opportunities for resilience, and integral threads in the evolving fabric of my faith. The church, once a static sanctuary of rigid answers, had become a dynamic space, a sacred theater where my spiritual journey unfolded, not in absolutes, but in the continual pursuit of understanding.

And in that pursuit, I discovered the essence of faith—not in having all the answers, but in embracing the sacred quest itself.

As the seasons changed, so did the landscape of my faith journey. Each Sunday, I walked through the familiar doors of the church—not in search of immediate answers, but with an open heart, ready to embrace the sacred quest unfolding both within and beyond those hallowed walls. The sermons, once an attempt to decode the mysteries of my life, became poetic narratives guiding me through the complexities of human experience. The verses, rather than serving as prescriptive solutions, became mirrors—reflecting the struggles, questions, and revelations of those who had walked this path before me.

Bible study sessions evolved into collaborative explorations, where diverse perspectives were not merely tolerated but celebrated. In sharing my vulnerabilities with fellow believers, I discovered the universality of human struggle—a bond that transcended doctrine and dogma. In those moments of collective introspection, I found not just a congregation, but a community—one bound not by a shared destination, but by a shared journey.

My struggles, though not erased, transformed. No longer obstacles to be overcome, they became catalysts for resilience, shaping me in ways I had never expected. Through the lens of faith, I no longer saw them as disruptions to a peaceful existence but as opportunities for growth, deeper understanding, and an expanded heart. The church, with its rituals and teachings, became less of a fortress and more of a compass—pointing me through the web of uncertainties, but never confining me within rigid walls.

My dialogue with faith shifted; it was no longer about seeking definitive answers, but about cultivating understanding and acceptance. The once-impossible distance between my spiritual aspirations and the realities of my life began to dissolve. I came to understand that faith was not a shield against hardship, but a lantern illuminating the path through it. My struggles, once seen as adversaries, became companions—teachers of patience, endurance, and grace.

As one chapter of my spiritual exploration ended, I found myself at the threshold of something new. I realized that the essence of faith lay not in possessing all the answers, but in the beauty of the sacred quest, a continuous unfolding, an invitation to explore the mysteries of existence with reverence and wonder.

No longer did I approach faith as a seeker grasping for certainty, but as a wanderer appreciating the melody of ambiguity. At the intersection of belief and uncertainty, I recognized that faith was not a static destination, but a dynamic journey—an ever-evolving composition, refining its notes with each passing day.

And so, with my spirit attuned to the sacred quest, I continued to return—not as a seeker expecting finality, but as a participant in the unfolding symphony of faith. Each note, whether joyous or sorrowful, contributed to the ever-changing melody of my journey. In the embrace of this sacred pursuit, I found something greater than answers—I found a profound appreciation for the beauty inherent in the mystery, the depth of the struggle, and the quiet, persistent whisper of His presence within my soul.

To the one seeking, questioning, and longing for clarity. Your journey of faith is not meant to be a straight path with easy answers; it is a sacred unfolding, a divine conversation between you and Yahweh that deepens with every step you take. The tension you feel between searching and understanding is not a sign of weakness, but of growth. The fact that you wrestle with these questions means your faith is alive, dynamic, and real.

Know this: **YAHWEH IS NOT INTIMIDATED BY YOUR DOUBTS.** He is not distant because you seek answers that seem just beyond reach. Instead, He is walking with you, patient and unwavering, guiding you through the mystery, not around it. Your hunger for understanding, your frustration in the waiting, and your longing for deeper truth are not in vain. They are all part of your refinement, drawing you closer to Him in ways you may not yet see.

The church is not the destination—it is a compass. The

Bible is not just a book of instructions—it is an invitation. Your faith is not meant to be stagnant; it is meant to grow, stretch, and transform as you do. The struggle does not mean you are lost; it means you are actively engaging in the most beautiful pursuit—the sacred quest for Yahweh's heart.

Let go of the pressure to have it all figured out. Embrace the mystery, the journey, the questions that don't yet have answers. Because faith is not about certainty—it is about trust. And trust means walking forward, even when you don't see the whole path.

KEEP SEEKING. KEEP ASKING. KEEP LEANING INTO HIS PRESENCE. He is not just waiting for you at the end of the journey—He is right beside you, whispering in the quiet, revealing Himself in ways beyond words. And as you continue this sacred quest, you will come to find that the beauty of faith is not in having every answer, but in experiencing the One who is faithful through it all.

Discovering His Heart

Discovering His Heart

CHAPTER 18
THE TUNNEL OF ENDLESS NIGHT

Discovering His Heart

That night, the room felt smaller than ever, as if the walls were conspiring to press in on me from all sides. The air was thick, burdened by the weight of a looming sunrise that seemed reluctant to arrive. A single song played on an endless loop, its melody imprisoned in repetition, a haunting soundtrack to my restless thoughts. The room became an island of self-examination, and though the music once felt like torment, it transformed into a strange solace—its familiarity a thread of continuity in a world that felt fractured. The lyrics, once mundane, took on new meaning with each cycle, mirroring the shifting layers of emotion unfolding within me. The relentless rhythm matched the pounding of my anxious heart, trapping me in a cycle I could neither escape nor fully embrace.

Dawn remained just beyond my reach, a taunting illusion that refused to materialize. Though I knew, rationally, that morning would come, the darkness clung stubbornly, swallowing any hint of approaching light. Time itself became distorted—both an ally and an adversary. The clock on the wall, unmoved by my desperation, seemed frozen, its hands locked in an indifferent embrace. Each second stretched into eternity, yet time itself refused to move forward, leaving me suspended in a limbo where the past and present blurred into one.

In the depths of this sleepless night, I found myself wrestling with the elusive nature of time. It was both measurable and ungraspable, relentless in its passing yet resistant to my longing for morning. Each tick of the clock echoed like a distant drum, marking the passage of time in a way that felt detached from my reality. I was caught in a paradox—longing for the night to end, yet trapped within its suffocating grasp.

And then, in the depths of this darkness, a vision took shape—the image of a tunnel, stretching endlessly before me, its entrance swallowed in an inky void. The whisper of an ancient tale stirred in my mind, daring me to walk through its depths in search of the guiding light.

The tunnel wrapped around me like a suffocating cloak, its walls cold and unyielding, echoing with the hollow sounds of my own footsteps. It was a corridor of shadows, a journey into the abyss. The air was heavy, dense with unspoken fears and the weight of unshed tears. The path ahead remained obscured, every step forward a blind leap into the unknown. The walls, if they could speak, would murmur stories of uncertainty, of silent battles fought within their confines. My own breath became a reminder of my loneliness, reverberating through the darkness like a solemn hymn to solitude.

It was a symphony of isolation, a melody composed of longing and loss. The tunnel became a metaphor for my internal struggles—I did not want to die; I just needed to see the light. The darkness was not merely an absence of illumination but a living force, consuming every flicker of hope that dared to emerge. It was a place of exile, where the outside world felt like a distant dream, where I was left alone with nothing but my thoughts.

There were moments when the weight of the darkness became unbearable, pressing against my very being, testing the limits of my endurance. Yet, in that crucible of sorrow, something unexpected emerged, a fragile but unbreakable will to keep moving forward. I realized that I did not need certainty to navigate the tunnel; I only needed the determination to take the next step.

As I fumbled through the tunnel's twists and turns, I encountered the remnants of my past—skeletons of regret, shadows of unfulfilled dreams. The walls bore witness to my history, forcing me to reckon with the echoes of the choices I had made. The tunnel was a mirror, reflecting the complexities of my existence, urging me to confront the truths I had long avoided.

And yet, even within the suffocating blackness, there were glimmers of resilience—a faint shimmer at the edge of my vision, whispering of the possibility of a different outcome. It was a fragile hope, but one that refused to be extinguished, a testament to the unyielding spirit within me.

The tunnel, for all its darkness, was also my only way out.

In the depths of the abyss, I found fragments of self-compassion, pieces of acceptance scattered like embers waiting to ignite. The darkness, once an enemy, became a teacher, revealing the hidden recesses of my soul. It was not just a passage of suffering but one of transformation, a journey where becoming was just as vital as arriving.

With every step forward, I carried the scars of this journey, each one a testament to resilience. The tunnel was unrelenting, but within its depths, I discovered an undeniable truth: the strength to find the light was already within me. And though the path remained uncertain, I knew one thing for certain—beyond the darkness, beyond the sorrow, a golden ray awaited.

Discovering His Heart

I closed my eyes, seeking refuge in the recesses of my mind, attempting to escape the weight of the moment. The boundaries blurred between the music and my thoughts, weaving a surreal symphony that mirrored the complexities of the night. Suspended in that space, I could almost taste the strange blend of anticipation and apprehension that hung in the air, thick and unmoving.

But as the night stretched on, something shifted. I became acutely aware of my own resilience—an unspoken strength quietly emerging within the chaos. My desperate yearning for daylight, once an unbearable ache, began to intertwine with a newfound acceptance of the present. Perhaps the night was not merely a prison but a passage, holding its own revelations and lessons.

With each cycle of the song looping endlessly in the background, a subtle transformation took place within me. The walls, though still confining, no longer seemed suffocating. The music, though repetitive, became a melody of endurance rather than torment. And the elusive tomorrow, still shrouded in mystery, now held the promise of renewal rather than dread.

Then, at last, the first timid rays of dawn pierced through the curtains, and with them came an overwhelming sense of release. The night, with all its weight and constraints, had become a narrative of resilience and introspection. The very walls that once seemed to close in had also borne witness to an evolution of my soul.

I climbed out from the depths of despair, stepping away from the precipice of my darkest thoughts, ready to meet the daylight that had finally conquered the relentless night. The clock, once a cruel tormentor, now stood as a silent witness to time's unyielding forward march—a quiet testament that even in the deepest darkness, the promise of a new day remains unwavering.

As the soft glow of morning bathed the room, the remnants of the night's struggle lingered like shadows—silent testaments to the endurance that had unfolded within those four walls. The once-oppressive space now carried a quiet serenity, as if the night had finally loosened its grip, granting passage into a realm of possibility. Outside, the garden stirred to life, the roses unfurling their petals in the warmth of daylight. The air carried a crisp freshness, gently washing away the weight of the hours before.

The same song that had played relentlessly through the night now faded into the background—a distant echo woven into the soundtrack of transformation. I took tentative steps toward the window, welcoming the gentle embrace of the sun, its golden rays casting a soft mosaic across the floor. The clock, once a cruel reminder of stagnation, now moved forward with quiet purpose, no longer an adversary but a companion on the journey into a new day.

Morning filled the room with the hush of renewal. The night, with all its confines and uncertainties, had become a crucible of resilience. The echoes of the once-repetitive song, once a torment, now whispered stories of endurance and self-discovery. In the aftermath of that long night, I carried with me the lesson that time's intricate dance held both confinement and liberation. The walls that had once seemed to close in had paradoxically expanded the boundaries of my understanding, proving that growth often emerges from the most unexpected places.

Stepping outside, the city of Ukiah moved with its usual cadence, oblivious to the quiet revolutions that had unfolded within the confines of that room. Yet, as I walked through its streets, the residue of introspection clung to me, a silent companion on my journey. The once-overwhelming bustle now mirrored the resilience I had discovered in solitude. The clock, no longer a tormentor, became a gentle guide—a reminder that time, however elusive, was an ally in the unfolding narrative of life.

The echoes of the night's song still lingered in the recesses of my mind, a refrain that sparked reflections on the cyclical nature of existence. Life, much like that sleepless night, moves through patterns of repetition and monotony—yet within those rhythms lie the potential for transformation.

In the heart of downtown Ukiah, I found moments of serenity—a sunlit park, a quiet café where time seemed to slow, the laughter of children in the background. Each moment carried the imprint of the night's endurance, a subtle reminder that even in the ordinary, profound revelations can be found. What I had learned in the crucible of that night became a compass, guiding me through the complexities of everyday life.

The desperate yearning for sunrise had softened into an appreciation of each passing moment. Tomorrow, no longer shrouded in uncertainty, stretched before me like a blank canvas, waiting to be filled with new experiences and endless possibilities.

Ukiah, with its chaotic symphony of life and the steady march of time, became a canvas for my ongoing journey, a journey shaped not only by the relentless ticking of the clock but also by the stillness that exists within the heart of a single, enduring night.

To the one who has walked through the longest night. You have endured what felt unbearable, stood in the silence when it screamed the loudest, and faced the shadows when they threatened to consume you. And yet, here you are. Still breathing. Still standing. Still moving forward.

The night was not your end; it was your passage. A place where you wrestled with time, with memories, with longing—but also a place where you discovered something deeper: YOUR OWN RESILIENCE. You have felt the weight of stillness pressing in, the ache of waiting for a dawn that seemed reluctant to come. And yet, morning came. It always does.

Let this be your reminder: YOU ARE NOT TRAPPED. The walls that once seemed to close in on you are not your prison, but your proof—that even when you felt confined, your spirit refused to be caged. That even when hope flickered, it never fully disappeared. That even in the deepest tunnel, YOU KEPT WALKING.

So take a breath. Step outside. Feel the warmth of the sun as it washes over you. It is yours. A gift, a promise, a quiet affirmation that you have survived another night, and with it, you are stepping into something new.

And the next time darkness lingers, remember this: YOU HAVE SEEN THE NIGHT BEFORE. And you have conquered it.

Discovering His Heart

CHAPTER 19
BROTHERHOOD IN THE MOUNTAINS

Discovering His Heart

Within the peaceful beauty of Pine Summit in Big Bear, a tapestry of souls converged for a spiritual retreat that transcended religious labels. Crafted with meticulous care by Valley Bible Fellowship Church, this retreat was more than an escape—it was a sanctuary for self-discovery, contemplation, and the sharing of life's most profound stories.

This was my first experience beyond the realm of business retreats and conferences, an uncharted path leading me into a brotherhood of men unafraid to unveil their innermost selves. In the refuge of this community, hearts unfolded, revealing the depths of both struggle and triumph. The serene landscapes of Pine Summit bore witness to a journey that was not just personal but collective, woven together through resilience, faith, and shared humanity.

From the moment I stepped into Pine Summit, I felt the embrace of something greater than myself. The lush greenery, the crisp mountain air—it all invited reflection. There was an energy in the air, a palpable blend of anticipation and fellowship, as men from all walks of life gathered under the covering of Yahweh. The retreat's schedule, carefully curated, balanced spiritual teachings, group activities, and moments of solitude.

As we settled into the rhythm of the retreat, walls—both physical and emotional—began to dissolve. What struck me most was the openness with which men shared their stories. It was a space free from judgment, where vulnerability was not just welcomed but encouraged.

In small circles, we spoke of our trials, career setbacks,

broken relationships, battles with addiction, struggles with faith. These were not merely personal confessions; they were threads in a greater tapestry, reminders that beneath the surface, we all wrestle with the same questions.

What unfolded was a profound realization: vulnerability was not a weakness but a source of strength. Men who had once been hesitant to expose their inner battles found solace in the collective honesty of the group. The retreat became a place to redefine masculinity—not through silence and self-reliance but through courage, emotional authenticity, and shared burdens.

In one particularly moving session, a man shared his struggle with mental health, breaking the silence around a subject often left unspoken. As he spoke, heads nodded, eyes welled with tears, and an unspoken truth settled over us—these struggles, though often hidden, were not meant to be faced alone.

At the heart of the retreat were teachings rooted in scripture, drawing from various chapters of the Bible. Yet, the messages transcended denomination—they resonated with a universal spirituality that called each man into deeper relationship with Yahweh.

Sermons, prayer, and reflective exercises wove seamlessly into our days, creating an atmosphere where faith was not just preached but lived. Conversations after services became extensions of these teachings, allowing for raw, personal interpretations that brought scripture to life.

Testimonies of triumph echoed through the retreat—stories of men overcoming addiction, restoring fractured relationships, and finding divine purpose in adversity. These were more than words; they were beacons of hope, reminders that even in the darkest moments, transformation was possible.

As we sat together, we exchanged practical tools for navigating life's obstacles—whether through community, counseling, or deepened spiritual practice. The retreat was not just an experience; it was a roadmap for overcoming hardship, a guide to faith-driven resilience.

With each passing day, a deep sense of brotherhood formed. Shared experiences, laughter, and even tears forged bonds that extended beyond the retreat center. In team-building exercises and group discussions, we discovered the power of unity—that strength was found not in isolation but in lifting one another up.

The retreat did not end at Pine Summit. Post-retreat support systems, including follow-up meetings and resources, ensured that the spiritual momentum did not fade. We were encouraged to carry this sense of brotherhood into our daily lives, to remain accountable to one another, and to continue walking in faith.

As the retreat ended, I found myself reflecting on the deeper meaning of this journey. In the days and weeks that followed, a realization took root in my heart—Yahweh had been orchestrating my path long before I set foot at Pine Summit.

The stories shared by the men, each a testament to His transformative power, became a mosaic of divine intervention.

Little did I know that through them, Yahweh was speaking to me, unveiling the boundless possibilities of a life surrendered to Him.

Through their testimonies, I saw reflections of my own journey—the struggles, the questions, the desire for redemption. The retreat became a vessel through which Yahweh revealed His presence, reminding me that even in my darkest moments, He had been there, shaping me for something greater.

In the aftermath of a painful divorce, I had often questioned my path. But through the openness of these men, I saw Yahweh's plan unfolding. They spoke of surrender—how relinquishing control had paved the way for unexpected blessings. Their testimonies encouraged me to trust that Yahweh was working in ways beyond my understanding.

I began to see my past not as a series of random events but as a carefully woven narrative in which Yahweh had been an active participant. Through the stories of restoration, healing, and redemption, I understood—my trials were not obstacles but opportunities for Yahweh to display His power.

As the retreat unfolded, hope penetrated the atmosphere. The testimonies of these men—of brokenness made whole, and despair turned into purpose—became guiding lights. They restored within me a flicker of faith, a belief that my journey was far from over.

These men, unknowingly, became vessels of His wisdom. Through them, He illuminated a path of surrender, faith, and unwavering trust. The retreat was a turning point—where

Discovering His Heart

Yahweh used the experiences of others to speak directly to my heart.

I left Pine Summit not just with memories, but with a renewed sense of purpose. I walked away knowing that Yahweh had been an active presence in my story long before I ever realized it. The retreat had become a sacred space where His presence was undeniable, His voice unmistakable, and His promises unshakable.

Valley Bible Fellowship Church's men's retreat was more than an event—it was a divine encounter, a moment where eternity touched time. Through shared vulnerability, unwavering brotherhood, and the undeniable presence of Yahweh, I found not just healing, but transformation.

As I stepped back into the world beyond Pine Summit, I carried with me a faith deepened by experience, a hope rekindled through testimony, and the certainty that with Yahweh, the journey ahead held boundless potential.

To the one who has walked this road. If you have felt the pull of something greater, if you have sat in the quiet of your soul and wrestled with purpose, if you have stood among brothers and found healing in shared stories—then know this: you are not alone.

There is a reason you were there, in that sacred space of openness and renewal. It was not by chance that your heart was stirred, that the words spoken resonated in the deepest parts of your being. Yahweh has been pursuing you, whispering through the testimonies of others, through the strength of brotherhood, through the moments when vulnerability became the doorway to freedom.

Your journey is not over. What was ignited in that retreat was not meant to stay in the mountains—it was meant to transform the way you walk through life. Hold onto what was revealed to you. Carry the lessons, the faith, the brotherhood into your everyday battles. Do not let the fire fade; instead, let it be the light that guides you through whatever comes next.

Even when doubts creep in, even when the weight of your past tries to pull you back, remember this: YAHWEH IS NOT FINISHED WITH YOU. He is working in ways beyond your understanding, turning your trials into testimony, your wounds into wisdom, and your pain into purpose.

So walk boldly. Keep seeking. Keep surrendering. Keep trusting. The same God who met you at Pine Summit is walking with you still, leading you into a future filled with restoration, strength, and unshakable hope.

YOU ARE SEEN. YOU ARE CHOSEN. YOU ARE NEVER ALONE.

Discovering His Heart

CHAPTER 20
THE CURRENCY OF COMPASSION

Embarking on my first venture into volunteer work at the local homeless shelter with our church's men's group was a mixture of eager anticipation and quiet apprehension. We arrived not only with trays of warm food but also with a burning desire to share the gospel, hoping to weave even the smallest thread of hope into the lives of those struggling against the harsh realities of street life. Our mission extended beyond the tangible offerings of hot meals; we sought to reach into the unseen spaces of the soul, bringing light to the shadows with faith and compassion.

As we gathered in front of the shelter, a collective heartbeat pulsed among us, an unspoken rhythm of empathy, bridging the divide between the fortunate and the struggle, between abundance and scarcity. The air carried the scent of warm food, mingling with something deeper—the weight of expectation, the hope that what we were about to do would mean something. Each tray was more than just sustenance for the body; it held a promise of friendship, understanding, and, perhaps, a fleeting moment of comfort for those living on the margins of society.

When the shelter doors opened, they revealed a world that ran parallel to our own yet was so often overlooked. Rows of beds stretched across the room, each occupied by a person with a story untold. The air was thick with emotion—resilience, struggle, and an underlying hope that someone, somewhere, still cared. As we set up tables with steaming plates of food, mostly donuts, I was struck by a wave of humility, tinged with sorrow. The blessings I often took for granted, simple, everyday comforts, were unattainable luxuries for many of the people before us.

Discovering His Heart

The men in our group moved with a shared sense of purpose, understanding that we were not just serving meals; we were offering dignity, connection, and the reassurance that these individuals were seen. When the doors finally opened to the waiting crowd, a diverse array of faces entered, each carrying the weight of a different hardship. Yet, what struck me most was not their suffering, but their gratitude. Their eyes held stories of pain, but also a quiet resilience, a deep appreciation not just for a warm meal but for the recognition of their humanity.

As we engaged in conversation, sharing the gospel in moments that transcended the walls of the shelter, I witnessed something powerful. It was not just about offering physical nourishment, it was about feeding the soul. I saw transformations unfold in the simplest exchanges: a handshake, a listening ear, a moment of genuine care. These interactions revealed a profound truth: gratitude is not measured by abundance but by awareness.

In those conversations, I learned more about strength, endurance, and faith than any sermon or self-help book had ever taught me. The people we met carried burdens that would break most, yet their spirits remained unbowed. Their thankfulness was not a mere courtesy, it was a testament to the human need to be acknowledged, to be valued, to be remembered.

Their smiles, their quiet words of appreciation, held a mirror to my own life, forcing me to confront the reality of my own privilege. Until that moment, I had not truly grasped the magnitude of their loss, nor the abundance in my own life. That evening, as we stepped away from the shelter, I carried more than an empty tray. I carried a lesson—one that would stay with me far beyond that night: the greatest gift we can offer is not just food or charity, but the willingness to see, to listen, and to love.

Leaving the shelter that day, the impact lingered. The experience became a catalyst for a profound shift in my perspective. I began to see my life through a new lens—one that illuminated the blessings I had so often overlooked. Gratitude, once just a concept, transformed into a living practice, woven into the fabric of my daily life.

Our men's group continued our volunteer efforts, not out of obligation but as part of a journey—one of mutual enrichment. The homeless shelter became more than a place of service; it became a sacred ground where stories intersected, where the act of giving transformed both the giver and the receiver. In those moments, I came to understand that true abundance was not measured by possessions but by the shared currency of compassion and gratitude.

In the weeks following my first visit, the resonance of that experience only deepened. Volunteering—whether at the shelter or in the streets on my own—became more than just an act of service. It was a journey of the soul, a pilgrimage into the empathy of Yahweh, shaping my understanding of His heart for the broken. As our men's group continued to serve meals and share moments of fellowship, relationships blossomed. The shelter was no longer just a refuge for the needy; it became a community woven together by the common thread of shared humanity.

Faces that had once been unfamiliar now carried names, stories, and a connection that transcended societal labels. Through these interactions, my understanding of gratitude underwent a profound transformation. No longer was it just a fleeting emotion—it became a daily choice, a conscious recognition of the abundance surrounding me.

The laughter and camaraderie that filled the shelter served as a powerful reminder that joy is not bound by circumstance. Even in the most unexpected places, light can break through. I found myself reflecting on the conversations we shared, the moments of hope, faith, and reassurance. The gospel, once something I had only spoken about, now felt alive. It was no longer just a message, it was an experience, an active force manifested in the warmth of a shared meal, in the sincerity of a listening ear, in the compassion that saturated the space.

That revelation changed me. Service was not just about what I could give; it was about what I could learn. Yahweh's love was not merely spoken—it was demonstrated. And in that realization, I found a greater calling—not just to serve, but to love as He loves, to see as He sees, and to live with a heart forever transformed by the depth of His grace.

Little did I know, the experience at the shelter was shaping a profound lesson for me, weaving threads of grace through both the lives of those we served and the struggles I had known myself. The shelter—meant to be a refuge for those the world often forgets—became my greatest teacher. Each time I stepped through its doors, my own brokenness found connection with those seeking shelter from life's storms. Faces worn by hardship, stories carved from resilience, it was a gathering of souls, each carrying a burden unseen by the outside world.

In this unlikely community, I began to recognize echoes of my own journey. The trials I had faced, though different, carried the same underlying theme—endurance through hardship. I saw faith in the unshaken perseverance of those who had lost so much, yet still clung to hope. The shelter taught me humility, just as I had once been reminded of the power of true hospitality. Sitting with people who owned little more than the clothes on their backs, I witnessed a generosity that transcended possessions. They welcomed me into their world, offering what little they had—a gesture that carried more significance than any grand offering ever could.

One woman, Beth, left a lasting impression on me. She shared her small meal with me, not out of abundance, but out of genuine selflessness. In that moment, I realized that generosity is not measured by quantity, but by the heart behind it. Her act of giving was a testament to the transformative power of compassion—proof that even the smallest gestures can carry immeasurable weight. In her face, I saw a reflection of the lesson that life had been trying to teach me all along—that strength is often found in the most unexpected places, that faith persists even in the midst of loss, and that kindness has the power to break barriers.

Before and after each gathering, we stood together in quiet moments of reflection. In those shared moments, I felt a connection beyond words—a collective plea for guidance, for provision, for hope. It reminded me of those who had walked uncertain paths before us, searching for direction, relying on unseen grace.

Through it all, I came to understand something I had not before: the shelter, at first a place where I thought I was offering help, had become a classroom for my soul. What I once saw as a space of absence revealed an abundance of wisdom, generosity, and the quiet strength of the human spirit.

In serving, I had come to be served—in a way that reshaped my perspective forever.

As the days turned into months, our men's group became more than just visitors at the homeless shelter—we became part of its heartbeat. My initial nervousness had given way to a shared anticipation, an unspoken understanding that whenever we gathered, something extraordinarily unfolded. The stories I once heard as tales of despair transformed into narratives of resilience and hope. The faces that had first appeared worn by hardship now carried imprints on my own journey, shaping the way I saw the world.

It was not that circumstances miraculously changed, but rather, my perspective had. I began to understand that service was never a one sided act. Yes, we brought meals to the shelter, but in return, the shelter nourished our souls. It became clear that giving had a ripple effect—one that extended far beyond the walls of that building. The shelter was no longer just a place of charity; it had become a sacred ground. It was where stories intertwined, where invisible wounds found healing, and where, despite life's ebb and flow, hope endured.

As we continued our mission, the shelter evolved into something greater than a place of refuge—it became a microcosm of shared humanity. Within its walls, differences faded, and harmonies developed. We were no longer just volunteers handing out meals; we were fellow travelers navigating the complexities of life, each carrying our own burdens and blessings.

Through open hearts and simple acts of kindness, quiet miracles unfolded. And in those moments, we came to understand that the greatest gift was not in what we gave, but in what we received—a profound lesson etched into the fabric of our collective journey.

What had once been a place of need had become an integral part of my personal transformation. It was there, among those the world often overlooked, that I learned an undeniable truth: until I embraced the struggles of others as part of my own story, I could never truly grasp the depth of gratitude. Their losses, once distant and abstract, became woven into the tapestry of my understanding, forever changing how I measured abundance, compassion, and the meaning of grace.

And so, my journey continued—each visit to the shelter, each shared meal on the street, another step deeper into the richness of gratitude. I discovered that in serving others, I was, in some way, serving myself. It was an unexpected dance—one where the more I gave, the more I received.

As I took tentative steps toward rebuilding my own life, I

found reflections of my story in the journey of the wanderer. The idea of return—of finding one's way back to belonging—became deeply personal. In the embrace of shared humanity, in the unguarded moments of connection, I sensed the quiet whisper of grace. It reminded me that no matter how far I had strayed, no matter the distance I had wandered, there was always a place for me.

And in that knowing, I understood that redemption is not found in grand gestures, but in the small, ordinary moments where love meets us exactly where we are.

To You, who has walked this path. If you have ever stood in a place where service turned into transformation, where giving became receiving, where you stepped into a space expecting to help but walked away forever changed—then you already know. You know that true impact isn't measured by the meals we serve or the words we speak, but by the moments of connection that linger in our souls long after we leave.

You have seen it—the resilience of those who have lost everything, yet still hold onto hope. You have felt it—the unspoken bond that forms when walls of judgment fall and we meet each other as human beings, not as giver and receiver, but as equals. You have witnessed it—the way Yahweh's love moves in spaces the world often overlooks, how His presence is felt in the quiet acts of kindness, in the simple exchange of a name, a handshake, or a moment of genuine eye contact.

And maybe, like me, you came to serve but found yourself being served. Maybe, in meeting those who have faced unimaginable hardship, you saw reflections of your own journey—the broken places, the unspoken struggles, the quiet battles fought in solitude. Maybe, through their gratitude, you were reminded of how much you have to be thankful for.

Let this be your reminder: YOUR PRESENCE MATTERS. What you did, what you continue to do, is not small. It is not insignificant. When you choose to see people, to truly see them, you are reflecting the heart of Yahweh Himself. In serving others, you are stepping into something sacred—something that stretches beyond charity and becomes an act of love, of healing, of redemption.

Keep going. Keep serving. Keep listening. Keep loving. The greatest impact you will ever have is not in what you give, but in how you allow yourself to be changed. This journey is shaping you in ways you may not even realize yet.

And if you ever wonder if it's enough—if the conversations, the meals, the moments of connection make a difference—know this: THEY DO.

You are walking in purpose. You are part of something bigger than yourself. You are exactly where you are meant to be.

Discovering His Heart

Discovering His Heart

CHAPTER 21
LESSONS FROM THE TANGERINE TREE
(RIP – SEPTEMBER 10, 1995)

Discovering His Heart

In the quiet sanctuary of the hospital yard, bathed in the warm hues of a setting sun, my father sat on a weathered bench—a silent guardian of resilience. His eyes, etched with the stories of a life well-lived, met mine with a quiet strength that spoke more than words ever could. It was a moment suspended in time, where the golden light softened the edges of years gone by, illuminating the face of a man who had braved life's storms and basked in its sunlit moments.

Beneath the sprawling branches of a tangerine tree, a sacred dialogue unfolded—a symphony of spoken words and unspoken understanding. It was a conversation about everything and nothing all at once, a mosaic of moments that had shaped him and, in turn, sculpted the very foundation of my own life. The bench, unassuming yet steadfast, became more than just a seat; it became an altar of shared experiences, a vessel cradling the echoes of a lifetime.

In the stillness, my father's voice wove stories of the past—tales stitched together with laughter and loss, triumphs and trials. Each word carried the weight of wisdom, painted in the rich hues that only time could blend. The bench bore witness, absorbing the quiet burden of unspoken emotions, becoming a confessional for the memories carved into the lines of his face.

As the sun dipped lower, stretching long shadows across the pavement, I discovered the magic hidden within the ordinary. It was in the way his hands moved, recounting a lifetime of labor and love. It was in the creases of his skin, each one a roadmap of the roads he had walked. My father did not merely share stories; he imparted something far more profound, the essence of resilience, the delicate art of navigating the labyrinth of life with grace. Our words flowed like a river, meandering through the valleys of reminiscence and rising to the peaks of wisdom. As my father spoke, the bench beneath us transformed—a vessel of quiet transformation, absorbing the joys and sorrows suspended in the air like a tender melody.

As the last rays of sunlight kissed the horizon, we rose from the bench, leaving behind a patchwork of conversations that lingered in the air like echoes of an unfinished melody. What was once a passing moment in time had become something sacred, the power of shared moments—where a father's wisdom met the eager heart of his child. And in that final exchange, as the twilight stretched its arms across the sky, we performed our last sacred dance—where mortality and eternity met, entwined in the quiet beauty of farewell.

As the bees engaged in a meticulous dance, they collected droplets of water with an almost sacred precision from the branches adorned with tangerine blossoms. Each bloom cradled a miniature reservoir, shimmering like liquid diamonds in the morning light. The air was alive with their rhythmic choreography—delicate wings humming in harmony with the rustling leaves. A mesmerizing spectacle unfolded before me—a mass of bees, draped in gold and black, moving with both purpose and grace. They navigated the intricate weave of petals, their movements a testament to nature's perfect design. Like masterful artists, they dipped into the heart of each blossom, savoring the fluid of life, turning the tangerine branches into a makeshift oasis.

Discovering His Heart

At that moment, my father turned to me, his gaze reflecting the weight of time—of experiences lived, lessons taught, and unspoken truths waiting to be revealed.

"I have taught you everything," he began, his voice carrying both the certainty of knowledge and the tenderness of regret. "Everything—except how to swim. That is my only regret."

I was taken aback by his words, a quiet mix of surprises and curiosity welling up inside me. Of all the things he had imparted, why swimming? Why this, of all the lessons left untaught? I looked at him, urging him silently to explain.

He exhaled, as if pulling the thought from deep within his soul.

"Swimming, my child, is not just about staying afloat in water. It is a metaphor for navigating the vast ocean of struggles that life will surely throw your way. I wish I had shown you how to swim—not just in water, but in the currents of challenges, uncertainties, and storms that will rise against you."

His words lingered in the air, settling into the spaces between us, heavy with meaning. I understood then that this was not about physical survival in water, it was about resilience, about learning to move with life's shifting tides rather than resisting them. And in that moment, as the bees continued their work among the blossoms, I realized the wisdom my father had carried all along:

Life is an unpredictable sea, and to survive, one must learn to swim—not just through water, but through the depths of adversity, the currents of change, and the storms that seek to pull us under.

In the days that followed, my father's words became my compass, guiding me through an unexpected curriculum, the school of life itself. Each interaction, each shared moment, became a lesson in staying afloat when adversity threatened to pull me under. Even the gentle waves lapping against the pier seemed to echo his teachings, a rhythmic reminder of life's ebb and flow.

There were moments of calm—days when the water mirrored a clear sky, when life unfolded smoothly, and I could simply glide. In those times, I remembered my father's words, savoring the stillness before the inevitable waves arrived. And when the storms did come, as they always did, I leaned on the lessons learned in those quiet moments—learning to stay afloat, to navigate through the chaos, and to emerge on the other side, stronger and wiser.

The years that followed brought their share of tempests—career uncertainties, personal losses, unexpected turns of fate. Yet, armed with the wisdom of that pivotal evening, I swam through them all with a newfound resilience. The ocean of struggles, once daunting, became a canvas for self-discovery and growth.

What had started as a survival skill had evolved into a philosophy, a way of approaching life with courage, embracing uncertainty, and riding the waves of change rather than resisting them. And in those moments of reflection by the ocean, I felt an unseen presence in the salty breeze, a quiet encouragement from my father's spirit, urging me to dive into life's challenges with the same quiet strength he had carried all along.

As the years flowed by, the metaphor of swimming continued to shape the contours of my journey. Life, like the ocean, held its own hidden beauty within the turbulence. But there was a pivotal moment, one that added an even deeper layer to this unfolding story, a moment that revealed how the wisdom passed from my father's lips was not merely an earthly teaching, but part of a divine plan that had been in motion long before I ever realized it.

To you, who has LOVED and LOST. Losing a parent is like losing a piece of the sky—something so vast, so constant, that you never imagined a day without it. The absence feels immeasurable, and grief comes in waves, sometimes gentle, sometimes overwhelming. But if you are reading this, if you have walked this road, then you already know—your love for them did not end when they left this world. It continues, woven into every lesson they taught, every memory they gifted you, every quiet moment where their presence still lingers.

Much like my father's wisdom about swimming, your parent left you with tools—lessons, love, and a strength you may not even realize you possess. Maybe they didn't prepare you for every wave life would bring, but their presence, their sacrifices, their unwavering belief in you—those were the strokes that carried you through the waters of life. And now, even in their absence, you are still moving forward, still learning how to swim.

Some days, grief will feel like an endless ocean, and you

may struggle to stay afloat. Other days, the tide will be calm, and you will remember them not just with sadness but with gratitude. Let those moments remind you that they are never truly gone. They live on in the lessons they left behind, in the resilience they passed to you, in the love that will never fade.

So when the waves crash, when the longing feels unbearable, remember: YOU ARE NOT ALONE. The strength they instilled in you—their wisdom, their love—will always be your lifeboat. And as you continue this journey, may you find comfort in knowing that every step you take, every challenge you overcome, is a tribute to the life they lived and the love they left behind.

You are swimming. You are surviving. And through it all, you are carrying them with you.

Discovering His Heart

CHAPTER 22
THE DISMANTLING OF A KINGDOM

Throughout my adult life, I was the captain of my own destiny, steering a grand vessel across the boundless seas of success. My sails were stretched wide, catching the winds of ambition, propelling me forward toward ever-greater heights. Life, as I saw it, was a magnificent feast of achievements, a table set with the finest rewards of my labor. I dined on the honors of a thriving career, a flourishing business, a grand residence, luxurious cars, and the radiant smiles of my two beautiful children.

I was the architect of my own triumphs, the maestro of a well-orchestrated symphony. In the competitive arenas of business and leadership, I carved out my place, holding executive positions that reflected my abilities—Director of Payroll, Human Resources, Analytics, CFO, and eventually CIO. Respected by my peers, I basked in the admiration that came with my accomplishments.

Yet, in the crescendo of my success, I failed to acknowledge the silent conductor of the universe—the genius beyond maestros. My ego drowned out the divine harmony that had made it all possible. I never once raised my eyes in gratitude, never humbled my heart to recognize the unseen force that had endowed me with gifts and talents.

But Yahweh, in His infinite wisdom, saw my heart drifting from His sacred path. The very gifts He had given me—meant to serve His purpose—had become instruments of my own self-glorification. I had helped build empires, not for His kingdom, but for the altar of my own pride. With every achievement, every accolade, I unknowingly placed another brick between myself and His divine blueprint for my life.

And so, with the precision of a master surgeon, Yahweh began the delicate process of removal. One by one, the pillars of my life began to shake. The thriving company I had helped build—the foundation of my professional pride—was struck by unseen tremors. The business I had meticulously crafted met with sudden storms, threatening to capsize the vessel I once believed was under my absolute control.

In the solitude of my despair, I stood before the wreckage of my ambitions. Despite my skills, my experience, and my once-unshakable confidence, I found myself in a storm without a compass. The empire I had built with my own hands crumbled around me, and for the first time, I stood powerless—adrift in the unpredictable currents of life, realizing that the captain's seat I had so firmly claimed was never truly mine to hold.

Home, once a sanctuary of warmth and love, now stood hollow, its walls whispering the echoes of loneliness. The splendor of my residence and the polished perfection of my cars had become ghostly reminders of a life built upon shifting sands. The respect I once commanded among colleagues faded into a distant echo, drowned beneath the growing tide of my own doubts. Yet, amidst the ruins of all I had built, a whisper stirred within the deepest chambers of my soul.

It was Yahweh. The unseen Maestro of my destiny, gently calling me to surrender my broken symphony and listen—to the melody He had composed all along.

I clung to the illusion that if everything else crumbled, my family would remain my anchor. But Yahweh, in His mysterious wisdom, stripped away even this final comfort. The bonds that once held my family together strained, unraveling thread by thread before my disbelieving eyes. The love that had once flowed freely, the foundation upon which I had built my sense of belonging, now faded like a vanishing tide, leaving me standing alone on the deserted shores of my existence.

"Why?" The question tore from my lips, carried away by the winds of despair.

"Had I not worked diligently, strived tirelessly, achieved abundantly? What cruel fate could unravel my world with such precision?"

And then, in the silence of my desolation, Yahweh revealed the answer—one that transcended human understanding. He had not taken everything from me out of cruelty, but out of love. It was a divine intervention, a precise and merciful surgery to remove the tumors of pride and self-reliance that had taken root within me.

Stripped bare, with nothing left to cling to, I found myself standing on the precipice of a spiritual journey, a demanding trek back to the Source I had unknowingly abandoned. The landscape before me was barren, and the path obscured by the shadows of my own doubt. Yet, beneath the weight of my losses, an undeniable pull remained—an invisible tether connecting my fractured soul to Him.

Loneliness wrapped around me like a heavy cloak as I stepped forward into the unknown. The echoes of my former life became distant whispers, drowned out by the profound stillness of surrender. Each step I took was a fragile balance between longing for the familiar and yielding to the sacred unknown—the place where I would either be lost completely or find what I had unknowingly sought all along.

In the stillness of my journey, I clung to fragments of my past like a shipwreck survivor grasping onto drifting debris. These remnants—shattered pieces of an identity I had once worn with pride—were woven together with threads of arrogance and self-reliance. Even as I stood at the edge of transformation, the struggle within me raged—a relentless tug-of-war between the comfort of the familiar and the call of something greater.

Though emptiness wrapped around me, I hesitated to relinquish the last remains of my former life. My ego, though wounded, refused to surrender fully. It whispered temptations of self-reliance, masquerading as dignity. The image of who I had once been clung to me like a phantom limb, haunting the hallways of my consciousness. But Yahweh, in His unshaken love, remained patient. His love was not conditional upon my readiness; it was steadfast, enduring, and unwavering in its pursuit of my heart.

And so, He orchestrated a symphony of events, composing each note with divine precision. He introduced people into my life, each one placed with purpose—to chip away at the final barriers guarding my soul. What seemed like chance encounters carried the fingerprints of the Almighty. Strangers became messengers, their words subtle yet piercing, delivering silent wisdom that resonated within the depths of my being. Like breadcrumbs leading me home, these moments guided me to a realization: surrender was not a loss but a rebirth.

Mentors appeared along the path, spiritual guides who carried light into the darkened corridors of my journey. Their presence was a testament to His relentless pursuit of my soul, their wisdom a salve to the wounds inflicted by my resistance. Slowly, I learned to walk again—much like an infant, unsteady yet determined. The journey, though isolating at times, became an intimate relationship with Yahweh, a sacred unfolding of trust and dependence.

In moments of stillness, I felt the gentle nudging of the Holy Spirit—a whisper that echoed through the valleys of my brokenness, inviting me to release the tattered remains of who I once was. It was a dance of grace, a choreography of redemption where even my faltering steps led me closer to the heart of Yahweh. The struggle, the resistance, the slow shedding of pride—all of it became part of a divine rhythm, a movement of surrender that, with each passing day, carried me deeper into the embrace of His unfailing love.

As I continued to surrender, little by little, I discovered an impossible strength hidden within the act of letting go. The battle I had once waged—between my will, my walk, and my desire to overcome—began to yield to a peaceful acceptance. It was an acceptance that whispered a profound truth: true strength is not found in resistance but in yielding to His will.

With each layer of my ego stripped away, I encountered feelings foreign to me—a metamorphosis that stretched beyond the limits of my understanding. This was not simply a return to Yahweh; it was a rebirth into a deeper knowing of His love. The journey became an intimate exploration, a pilgrimage into the sacred chambers of His heart.

Even in the solitude, His love manifested in unexpected ways. A sunrise became a gentle reminder of His daily grace. The kind words of a friend became a soothing melody against life's harshness. The ordinary became extraordinary as I began to recognize His fingerprints in every detail of my existence.

With time, I came to see how Yahweh had woven together a tapestry of grace—each event, each encounter, a thread leading me back to Him. My journey's purpose was no longer found in a final destination but in the unfolding revelation of His character, a character defined by relentless love, boundless compassion, and an unwavering pursuit of my reckless soul.

At times, I retraced the terrain of my past, standing amidst the ruins of who I once was. I saw the ashes of ambitions, the fragments of shattered dreams, and the echoes of a prideful past. And yet, in that reflection, I understood the beauty of what had been removed. Yahweh's divine surgery had not been an act of cruelty but one of mercy—stripping away the veneer of worldly success to reveal something far more sacred beneath.

With every step, my journey became a sacred dialogue. I questioned. I wept. I longed for understanding. And Yahweh, in His infinite patience, did not answer with thunderous proclamations but with the rustling of leaves, the hush of a breeze, the still, small voice that assured me His heart remained open to the broken and the repentant.

The loneliness that had once felt oppressive transformed into solitude filled with His presence. What I had once perceived as emptiness was no longer a void to be feared but a canvas upon which Yahweh painted the masterpiece of my redemption.

And so, with every step closer to Him, I shed not only the remains of my former life but also the burdens of my own misconceptions. The journey was never about reaching perfection. It was about embracing imperfection with the understanding that His love was never contingent on my achievements—it was found in my willingness to surrender. Fully. Unconditionally. Completely.

During my journey home, I began to fathom the depths of His heart, a heart that pulses with love, forgiveness, and an unquenchable desire for relationship with His creation. The removal, orchestrated with divine precision, was never a punishment; it was a rescue mission—a mission to reclaim my wandering soul and bring it back into the folds of His grace.

As I neared the threshold of surrender, I realized that this journey was never meant to be walked alone. In His mercy, Yahweh placed fellow travelers on my path—kindred souls who carried their own stories of redemption. Together, we formed a fellowship bound not by status or success, but by surrender. We learned that true strength is not found in power or control, but in vulnerability—in the willingness to admit our need for something greater than ourselves.

With each step, the emptiness that once terrified me became the very space where Yahweh's presence became tangible. In the void, I was no longer abandoned but embraced. The removal of the world I had so meticulously constructed was, in reality, an unveiling of grace. I was never alone. Every breath, every heartbeat, was a testament to His enduring love.

The dark night of my soul became a canvas upon which Yahweh painted the masterpiece of redemption. In the echoes of my shattered dreams, I heard His whispers of guidance. In the breaking down of everything I had once clung to, I saw His mercy at work.

This was not destruction for the sake of ruin; it was a sacred dismantling, a breaking down of the ego-forged walls that had long separated me from the purpose for which I was created.

As I stood in the debris of my former life, I finally understood. The removal was not an end but an invitation, an invitation to rebuild, not upon the shifting sands of worldly success, but upon the unshakable foundation of faith. The broken pieces of my past were not discarded but repurposed, becoming the fertile soil where humility, gratitude, and surrender could take root.

And in my surrender, I began to gain what I had never truly possessed, the richness of spiritual awakening, the depth of genuine connection, and a purpose no longer dictated by my own ambition but co-authored by the One who had been guiding me all along. My talents were never meant for self-glorification, but for service. The career, the business, the possessions, all the things I once held in such high regard—were mere instruments, not the conductor of the orchestra.

Yahweh, in His patient love, had orchestrated a divine

intervention to recalibrate my life's melody—to bring my soul back in tune with the harmonious chords of His divine purpose. And in the absence of worldly distractions, I finally found what had been missing all along.

In prayer, I found comfort. In silence, I heard His voice—soft, steady, ever-present. His guidance had always been there, waiting beneath the noise of my ambitions. It was a communion beyond words, a dialogue not of desperation, but of belonging—a conversation between a broken soul and an omnipotent Creator.

And in that sacred stillness, I knew I had finally come home.

At the peak of my journey, I knelt before Yahweh—not as a conquered servant, but as a beloved child. The removal, the loneliness, the battles within—all had been part of His divine alchemy, transforming my heart, refining my soul. I had come to see Yahweh not only in the grandeur of creation but in the intricate details of my life, woven with purpose and intentionality.

The removal was never meant to strip away my identity but to reveal my most authentic self, the one intricately designed for His eternal plan. As I remained before His throne of grace, I understood that my journey was not one of arrival, but of continual becoming. The process of refinement was ongoing, a sacred cycle of shedding the old and embracing the new, of surrendering what was never truly mine to receive what had always been meant for me.

And so, with my heart now attuned to the sacred rhythm of

surrender, I stepped into a new chapter, one where my identity was no longer tethered to titles, achievements, or possessions, but to the profound truth that I was, above all else, a beloved creation of the Almighty.

What I had once perceived as a tragedy, I now recognized as a gateway, a passage leading me into a life immersed in divine purpose, one that transcended the fleeting pursuits of the world. As I rebuilt from the ashes, my focus shifted from accumulation to contribution. The talents I had once wielded for personal ambition now became instruments of service, dedicated not to self-glorification but to uplifting others.

The definition of success has changed. No longer measured in wealth or prestige, it was found in purpose—using resources to support the less fortunate, applying my skills to create meaningful impact, and leveraging technology for the greater good. The grand house and luxurious cars were replaced by a humble home and a modest vehicle—not as a sign of loss, but as a symbolic shedding of the excesses that once defined my worth.

In the simplicity, I found abundance. In the surrender, I found freedom. In the removal, I found Yahweh.

In the sacred spaces of gratitude, I thanked Yahweh not only for the blessings but for the trials. For it was in the trials that I discovered the depths of His mercy, the unwavering strength of His love, and the transformative power of His grace. Where once pride had ruled in the quiet chambers of my heart, humility now blossomed, a humility born from the realization that every breath, every heartbeat, was His gift.

Discovering His Heart

I had been given a second chance—not to live for myself, but for the One who had orchestrated my existence with love and purpose. The story of the removal was not a tragedy; it was a triumph. A triumph of the soul over the illusions of worldly success. A triumph of His love over the fleeting pleasures of the material world. The scars left by the dismantling were not wounds of defeat but badges of honor—reminders of a journey through the crucible of transformation.

And so, with my heart humbled and my spirit near full surrender, I stood on the edge of a new beginning. I understood then—what had been stripped away was not the end but a genesis. The tapestry of my life, rewoven by the hands of grace, bore witness to an orchestra—one that no longer played the discordant tolls of worldly ambition but instead resonated with the beautiful melody of divine purpose.

Like a Kintsugi bowl, my brokenness had been mended with gold, each fracture now lined with the brilliance of His redemption. The pieces of my past had not been discarded, but reshaped, transformed into something even more beautiful, even more whole, because of the breaking.

The removal, though painful, was a revelation—an unveiling of the eternal truth that in surrendering to Yahweh, I had not lost, but gained. It was the catalyst for my awakening—an awakening to the profound truth that in losing everything, I had found my truest self.

In surrender, I gained the infinite riches of His love. And in that love, I discovered the most precious treasure of all—the intimate relationship with the heart of Yahweh.

To you, who has walked this road. If you have felt the ground shift beneath you, if you have watched the empire you built crumble into dust, if you have been stripped of everything you thought defined you—know this: YOU ARE NOT ALONE.

I know the pain of losing control, of standing before the wreckage of your past, wondering where Yahweh is in the midst of it all. I know what it feels like to grip tightly onto the last remnants of pride, only to realize that Yahweh, in His mercy, is gently unclenching your fingers, asking you to let go.

But hear me when I say—THIS IS NOT THE END.

What feels like devastation is, in reality, the hand of a loving Father, stripping away what was never meant to sustain you, so He can give you something far greater. The removal is not His wrath—it is His rescue. He is not tearing you down to destroy you; He is refining you to restore you. Every loss, every breaking, every tear is a thread in the tapestry He is weaving—a masterpiece of redemption that only He can create.

It is in the surrender that you will find your true strength. It is in the letting go that you will finally take hold of what truly matters. And it is in the stillness, when all else has been taken, that you will hear His voice more clearly than ever before.

Your identity is not in what you build, but in WHO YAHWEH SAYS YOU ARE. Your worth is not in titles, wealth, or status, but in the UNSHAKABLE TRUTH THAT YOU ARE HIS.

So, if you are standing in the ruins, wondering what comes next, know this: YAHWEH IS NOT FINISHED WITH YOU. What you have lost is nothing compared to what He is preparing for you. Step forward, not in fear, but in faith. He has already written your redemption story, and the next chapter is about to unfold.

YOU ARE SEEN. YOU ARE LOVED. AND IN HIS HANDS, YOU ARE BEING MADE NEW.

If these words resonate with you, if you find yourself standing among the ruins of what once was, wondering how to move forward—take heart. Yahweh has not abandoned you. What feels like the unraveling of your life is actually the beginning of something greater. The stripping away is not to harm you but to heal you. The breaking is not to destroy you but to build you into who He always intended you to be.

Remember, Yahweh is the Master Potter, and sometimes the clay must be reshaped, refined, and even broken to become the vessel He has destined it to be. The fire of refinement is painful, but it is necessary to remove impurities, to bring forth something pure, strong, and unshakable.

So, do not fear the loss. Do not cling to the ashes of what once was. Instead, open your hands. Let go. Trust that what He is doing is beyond what you can see now. His plans are higher than yours, and His ways are greater than your understanding.

This is not your end—this is your beginning. Yahweh is making a way where there seemed to be none. He is turning your sorrow into joy, your mourning into dancing. Keep your eyes fixed on Him, for He is faithful. Even in the silence, He is working. Even in the waiting, He is moving.

Stand firm. Keep walking. What is ahead of you is greater than what is behind you. Yahweh is your refuge, your restorer, your redeemer. You are not forsaken. You are His. And in His hands, you are being made new.

Discovering His Heart

CHAPTER 23
THE SACRED SURRENDER

In the gentle background of sunlight beyond my window on that fateful August afternoon, I stood at the sacred intersection of desperation and sincere surrender. August 21, 2023—a date now engraved in the chronicles of my life, marking the moment I willingly released the reins of control, laying the fractured pieces of my existence before the divine gaze of the Almighty.

I laid bare my struggles, my fears, and my dreams at the feet of Yahweh, placing my trust in a force far greater than myself to guide me through the maze of life. The weight of my burdens, the echoes of past achievements reduced to ashes, and the relentless storms of existence had worn me down. I was not merely tired; I was depleted, stripped of the strength to endure another day.

With my back pressed firmly against the wall, I retreated to my bed, a sanctuary that had become the silent witness to my unraveling soul. In the cradle of my vulnerability, tears broke free like a river surging through shattered barriers. I cried out—not with the echoes of arrogance that once shaped my prayers, but with the raw, unfiltered honesty of a broken spirit.

The words poured from the depths of my being, a desperate plea:

"Yahweh, I am a sinful man. I did everything I possibly could, but nothing worked. I am out of options. You are all I have. I don't want anything else but You."

My room, dimly lit by golden rays of the setting sun, transformed into a sacred chamber where my cries resonated with the weight of surrender. My bed became an altar, bearing witness to the final laying down of my self-sufficiency.

On my knees, my forehead resting against the golden wooden floor, my palms turned upward, my tears became my only offering. The last remnants of my pride slipped away as I gave Yahweh everything—the broken, the lost, the defeated.

It was a prayer not shaped by eloquence, not crafted with thought, but one born of desperation. A plea that transcended human understanding, reaching into the heavens—a soul's final surrender to the only One who had ever truly been in control.

And then, in the hallowed silence that followed my cry, something shifted—a subtle yet profound change. It was not a thunderous response from the heavens, no dramatic sign carved into the sky. Instead, it was a quiet assurance, a presence so gentle yet undeniable, wrapping around me like a comforting cloak. It was as if the divine itself had stepped into the room, filling the space with a peace that surpassed all understanding.

In that moment, I let go. Completely.

The weight of my striving, the illusion of control, the shattered remnants of my plans—I released them all. The cradle of my despair became the womb of my rebirth. For the first time, I was no longer fighting, no longer clinging to what was already broken.

Instead, I placed my fractured heart into the hands of the One who had been waiting all along.

There, in the simplicity of surrender, I gave Yahweh the

reins to my life, my purpose, my very being. And in return, Yahweh, in His infinite grace, bestowed upon me the one thing my soul had unknowingly longed for all this time—a deep and unshakable connection with Him.

It was not a material blessing, nor a swift resolution to my earthly problems. It was something far greater—the gift of His heart. An assurance that in surrendering to Him, I had gained the most precious treasure of all.

My tears, once flowing from desperation, transformed into rivers of gratitude. The room, once a chamber of brokenness, became a sanctuary of divine embrace, a sacred space where the Holy Spirit met my weary soul with open arms.

I was home.

Following that sanctified moment of surrender, a cascade of events unfolded, events that defied logic, moments that bore witness to the benevolence of Yahweh, who hears the cries of His children. It marked the beginning of a journey—one not without trials, but one where divine providence guided every step.

In the days and weeks that followed, I became profoundly aware of His hand, orchestrating the symphony of my life. Doors that had once been sealed shut swung open with a gentle breeze of opportunity. Challenges that once loomed as insurmountable obstacles became steppingstones—lessons in growth, in resilience, in trust.

That pivotal moment of full surrender on August 21,

2023, was more than a cry for help—it was a birthing cry, a declaration of new life. It was the turning point in my story, the moment when I truly understood that in my weakness, His strength was made perfect. Surrender was not the end of my striving—it was the beginning of my becoming.

In the unfolding journey that followed, the tapestry of His wisdom became evident, each event and encounter a carefully woven thread in His grand design. Yahweh, the Master Weaver, was crafting something beyond my understanding—a narrative filled with purpose, one that reflected the deepest desires of my heart, even those I had never spoken aloud.

My journey continued, not absent of trials, but with the unwavering assurance that the One who heard my cry on that sacred night would guide my every step. The removal, the surrender, and even the unexpected blessings that followed were all part of His divine story—a narrative that echoed the eternal truth: when I give Yahweh everything, He, in turn, fulfills the deepest desires of my heart.

But in the progressing pages of my life, I came to realize that the greatest gift was not the restoration of possessions, nor the resolution of earthly struggles. The greatest gift was intimacy—the unbreakable bond forged in the crucible of surrender, a relationship with Yahweh that transcended the fleeting pursuits of the world.

And so, with a heart now attuned to the rhythms of His grace, I embraced the continuing journey. I came to understand that surrender was not a single moment, but a daily practice, a constant realignment of my will to His.

Discovering His Heart

The removal, the tears, and the surrender were never meant to be an ending. They were the beginning. An introduction to a life where every breath, every step, bore testimony to the transformative power of His redeeming heart and His boundless, unconditional love.

And now, as the morning sun painted the sky with the promise of a new beginning, I understood.

I had not been abandoned. I had been pursued.

Yahweh had been leading me all along—not to break me, but to restore me. To take the ashes of my past and turn them into something beautiful. To show me that my worth had never been in what I could do, but in who I was—His son.

THE WAR WAS OVER. THE STRIVING HAD CEASED. I WAS HOME.

To you, who has stood at the crossroads of desperation and surrender. If you have ever reached the end of yourself, if you have cried out to Yahweh in the depths of your brokenness, if you have released control with trembling hands, then know this: YOU ARE NOT ALONE.

I see you. More importantly, HE SEES YOU.

Surrender is not the end—it is the beginning. It is not a mark of failure, but the doorway to transformation. The moment you give Yahweh everything, you step into the vastness of His love, into the safety of His embrace.

You may still feel the weight of what you have lost, the ache of what once was, but trust this: Yahweh does not remove without purpose. He does not allow breaking without the promise of restoration. What you have surrendered into His hands is not abandoned; it is being REBUILT, REFINED, AND REDEEMED in ways beyond what you can yet see.

The night you cried out, heaven heard you. The weight you released, Yahweh carried. And the path before you? It is no longer yours to walk alone. You are HELD, GUIDED, AND LED BY THE ONE WHO HAS BEEN PURSUING YOU ALL ALONG.

So, step forward—not in fear, but in faith. The war is over. The striving has ceased. You are home in Him. And THIS IS ONLY THE BEGINNING.

And now, as you stand on the threshold of something new, know that Yahweh is not just leading you forward—He is walking beside you, every step of the way. What was once heavy was lifted. What was once uncertain, is now held in His perfect plan. You are no longer bound by the burdens of yesterday, nor defined by the pain of what was lost. You are being made new.

Rest in this truth: Yahweh's hands are steady, His grip on you is firm, and His love is unfailing. Your surrender was never about losing—it was about gaining something far greater. In His presence, you are not forgotten. You are chosen. You are beloved. You are strengthened for what's ahead.

So take courage. Step forward with expectation. What

Yahweh is preparing for you will not only restore what was lost, but will surpass anything you could have imagined. This is not just the beginning—it is the unfolding of a testimony that will declare His faithfulness, power, and love. The road ahead is paved with grace. Walk boldly, for Yahweh has already gone before you. THIS IS YOUR TIME TO RISE.

Discovering His Heart

GRATITUDE

Dearest Jen,

I want to take a moment to express my deepest gratitude for the incredible gift you gave me—the Overcomer Journal. It has been a beacon of light in my life, and I cannot thank you enough for the impact it has had on my journey.

From the moment I opened its pages, I felt a profound sense of empowerment and courage to begin writing my story. Your thoughtful gesture provided me with a sacred space where I could freely express my thoughts, emotions, and the remarkable journey I have walked. More than just a journal, it became a sanctuary—a place where I could process my triumphs, struggles, and the faithfulness of Yahweh in my life.

I want to acknowledge and appreciate the haven you have created for me. It takes a special person to extend such a gift, and you have done so with grace and warmth. Your unwavering support has given me the courage to be vulnerable, to share both the victories and the challenges I have faced. Through your kindness, I have found the strength to open my heart and testify to what Yahweh has done in my life.

The countless hours you have spent listening to my stories, walking through each chapter with me, and sharing in both laughter and tears have made this journey even more meaningful. Your presence has been a source of comfort, and I am deeply grateful for the genuine connection we have forged through this process.

As I reflect on my journey with the Overcomer Journal—where Discovering the Father's Heart took shape, I am reminded of a powerful passage from Scripture:

"The righteous cried out, and Yahweh heard, And delivered them out of all their distresses. Yahweh is near to the brokenhearted, And saves those whose spirit is crushed." —Psalm 34:17-18 (ISR)

Our stories, much like those in the Bible, are woven with moments of trial and triumph, sorrow and hope. I see the parallels between my journey and those of individuals in Scripture who faced adversity yet emerged stronger through faith and resilience.

Just as Moses led the Israelites through the wilderness, you have been a guiding presence, helping me navigate life's uncertainties. Like Joseph, whose story of betrayal and hardship ultimately led to redemption, your kindness and wisdom have reminded me of the power of forgiveness and the triumph of grace. And like David, who went from shepherd to king by trusting in Yahweh's plan, your encouragement has been a steadfast reminder to trust in the unfolding of my own story, knowing that His plans are far greater than I can imagine.

Thank you for being a living reflection of Yahweh's love and compassion. Your support has been a tangible expression of His grace in my life. As I continue to write and share my story, I draw strength from the resilience of those who have walked before me and find comfort in the beautiful connection of our journeys.

You have been a beacon of light—encouraging me, listening with compassion, and making a lasting impact on my path of healing and discovery. For that, I am forever grateful.

May we continue this journey of faith, resilience, and victory together. May Yahweh's joy and blessings overflow in your life.

With heartfelt thanks and all my love,

Timothy T. Saipramuk "Mai Thai"

Discovering His Heart

My Beloved Children,

As I write these words in Discovering the Father's Heart, my soul is filled with a deep sense of purpose—one rooted in the desire to share with you the journey I have walked. A journey of seeking purpose, navigating the currents of life, and ultimately discovering the unwavering love that flows from the heart of Yahweh.

As you both continue to grow into the remarkable individuals Yahweh created you to be, I know there may come moments when questions arise. Perhaps you've wondered why Daddy was often away during your tender years. My loves let me unravel this mystery through the threads of our family story and the eternal truths woven into the sacred verses of Scripture.

Proverbs 3:5-6 (ISR) remind us: "Trust in Yahweh with all your heart, And lean not on your own understanding; In all your ways acknowledge Him, And He makes your paths straight."

It was this trust that guided me every step. The choices I made were not out of selfish ambition but were deeply rooted in faith—anchored in the unwavering belief that Yahweh was unfolding a greater purpose, one intricately woven into the fabric of our lives.

Psalm 37:5-6 (ISR) offers us comfort: "Commit your way to Yahweh, And trust in Him, and He does it. And He shall bring forth your righteousness as the light, And your right-ruling as midday."

Each sacrifice, each moment of separation, was offered with a steadfast heart, knowing that Yahweh was leading me to build a foundation for our future. My prayer has always been that your lives would be bathed in His abundant blessings at the dawn of each new day, just as He declared in Genesis 1:28 (ISR): "And Elohim blessed them, and Elohim said to the, 'Be fruitful and increase, and fill the earth and subdue it, and rule over the fish of the sea, and over the birds of the heavens, and over all creeping creatures on the earth.'"

I want you to remember, my darlings, that life unfolds in seasons. Ecclesiastes 3:1 (ISR) reminds us: "For every matter there is an appointed time, even a time for every pursuit under the heavens."

Those moments of absence were but a season, a chapter in the greater story of our family. Every challenge, every sacrifice, was in harmony with Yahweh's divine timing, paving the way for the fulfillment of His plans for us.

As you journey through the pages of Discovering the Father's Heart, may you find answers to the questions that have lingered in your hearts. Life is a sacred journey, and every step—no matter how difficult, shapes the tapestry of who we are.

My greatest hope is that together, we will continue this exploration of the heart—the heart of our family, the foundation of our faith, and, above all, the infinite and unshakable love of Yahweh.

With all my love,

Daddy

Discovering His Heart

My sister Pon and my brother Brian,

As I sit down to pen these words, my heart overflows with gratitude, admiration, and a profound sense of appreciation for the two extraordinary individuals who have been my pillars of strength throughout life's journey.

As we navigate the tapestry of time, I find myself reflecting on our shared history—marked by challenges and triumphs, laughter and tears. In the absence of our beloved father, who passed away in 1995 in Thailand, our path has been one of resilience, unity, and unwavering love.

Today, I want to express my deepest gratitude to both of you for being the constants in my life, for your encouragement, your love, your support, and for being unwavering anchors during the storms we faced. Growing up without the guiding presence of our father was undoubtedly a challenge, but it was through your resilience, courage, and steadfast support that we not only endured but emerged stronger, united and deeply bonded as a family. Each of you played an irreplaceable role in shaping the person I am today, and for that, I am profoundly thankful.

Pon, where do I begin? Your presence in my life has been nothing short of a blessing. Your strength and resilience have been a guiding light in my darkest moments. The grace with which you have navigated life's challenges and your unwavering commitment to our family have left an indelible mark on my heart.

Thank you, Pon, for being my rock, my confidante, and my greatest supporter. Your love has been a constant, surpassing both time and distance. No matter what life brought our way, your unwavering spirit and boundless love were a beacon of hope and strength. What stands out most is your incredible ability to extend your hand each time I stumbled and fell. Your support was never conditional, your encouragement never contingent on success. You were there—selfless and wholehearted—ready to lift me up and guide me through the darkest hours.

There were times when the weight of the world seemed unbearable, moments when I questioned my own strength. But in those times, it was your hand that reached out, your comforting words that echoed in my ears, and your unwavering belief in my potential that transformed my despair into determination. Your love, Pon, has been a source of healing and empowerment, and for that, I am eternally grateful.

Brian, my dear brother, you are a living testament to the power of familial bonds. Your quiet strength, resilience, and unspoken support have been the foundation upon which our family stands tall. From the laughter of shared childhood memories to the steadfast courage you show in the face of adversity, your presence has been a source of comfort and reassurance.

During life's storms, when everything seemed uncertain, your calm demeanor and steady presence were the anchors that kept us from drifting. Your unwavering commitment to our family's well-being has been a guiding light, a reminder that no matter how turbulent the journey is, we are never alone. Together, we have faced trials, celebrated victories, and woven a tapestry of shared experiences that form the very fabric of our lives.

To both of you, my sister and brother, I want to emphasize that your love and support have not only shaped my personal journey but have also woven a powerful story of family resilience. Through every hardship and victory, you have exemplified the true essence of familial love—selfless, enduring, and unconditional. I acknowledge the sacrifices you both have made, the countless times you put our family's well-being above your own, and the unwavering love that has been the cornerstone of our shared life. Your resilience has been a beacon of hope, your love a constant in the ever-changing landscape of life.

With a heart full of gratitude and love,

Your Brother

Discovering His Heart

Discovering His Heart

ABOUT THE AUTHOR

Meet Timothy T. Saipramuk, a courageous seeker who embarked on a profound journey through the wilderness, searching for the answer to life's deepest question: Why?

After experiencing profound loss, he spent four years in the vast, untamed expanse of the wilderness, confronting the rawest depths of his soul. Each day was a battle—a relentless war against doubt, despair, and the overwhelming weight of grief. His will to live lay in ruins, shattered by the storm raging within. The voice of doubt, like a relentless specter, whispered fear and uncertainty into his mind, challenging the very foundation of his faith. Suspended by a fragile thread, he wrestled with its meaning, questioning its relevance in a world that seemed determined to break him.

Then, on September 24, 2023, destiny intervened. Jen Horling, visionary founder of The Overcomers, recognized the resilience within him and gifted him the Overcomers Journal, urging him to write his story. The following morning, Timothy put pen to paper for the first time, beginning with two simple yet profound words: "Unanswered Questions."

His journey is more than personal triumph—it is a testament to the power of faith, resilience, and redemption. Through his writing, Timothy does not just tell his story; he shares the story of somebody who reached into the depths of his suffering and saved his soul. Now, he seeks to ignite that same hope in others, proving that even in the darkest moments, light can break through for those who dare to seek it.

Discovering His Heart

WE'D LOVE TO HEAR FROM YOU!

Have a testimonial from reading? Please share it here;

Then scroll down to the bottom where it says *customer reviews* on the far right and click **"write a customer review".**

Email us at:

info@theovercomersmovement.com

www.theovercomersmovement.com

Find us on Social Media:

Facebook: @WeBelieveInYourStory
Instagram: @Overcomers_filledwithgold

FREE DOWNLOAD

Cheat Sheet to Overcoming the Next 12 Months

Submit Email

www.theovercomersmovement.com

FREE GROUP

Monthly Hunt for Gold

Find us on Facebook!

Join Here

HELP US HELP OTHERS

Overcomer Kits

Sent to families who have lost someone they loved to suicide

Submit a name

Donate & help us send more kits

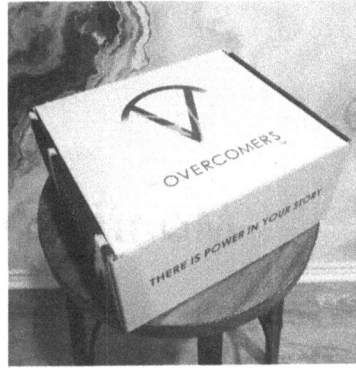

OTHER BOOKS BY THE OVERCOMERS

"Finding His Voice"

Available on Amazon.
Scan QR Code:

"Finding His Timing"

Available on Amazon.
Scan QR Code:

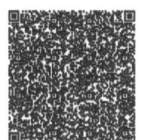

www.ingramcontent.com/pod-product-compliance
Lightning Source LLC
Chambersburg PA
CBHW011521070526
44585CB00022B/2490